Postmodern
Indian English Literature

Bijay Kumar Das

ATLANTIC
PUBLISHERS & DISTRIBUTORS (P) LTD

ATLANTIC
PUBLISHERS & DISTRIBUTORS (P) LTD
7/22, Ansari Road, Darya Ganj, New Delhi
Tel.: +91-11-4077 5252, 2327 3880
E-mail: orders@atlanticbooks.com
Web: www.atlanticbooks.com

Published by Atlantic Publishers & Distributors (P) Ltd., 2024
Reprint 2006, 2010, 2013, 2022, 2024

Printed & bound in India by Atlantic Print Services

Preface

Indian English Literature has a luxuriant growth in the post-1980 period. It has an all-round development unprecedented in the literary history of our country. Indian English poets and fiction writers have won world-wide acclaim during 1980s and afterwards. In my book, I have made an attempt to present the literary history of Postmodern Indian English Literature critically before the readers. Since this book is a critical survey of the history of Indian English Literature in the post-1980 period, it has its shortcomings—for no book of history of literature can be perfect. But, nevertheless, I have made an effort to evaluate the trends in Indian English literature genre-wise—poetry, fiction, short story, drama and autobiography—so that, this book can serve as a book of introduction to Indian English literature from 1980 to the present-day. As usual, a bibliography has been given both by way of acknowledgment and by way of bringing to the notice of the readers the materials available in the field.

Last but not the least, I am thankful to M/s Atlantic Publishers and Distributors, New Delhi, particularly to Dr K.R. Gupta, its Managing Director, for bringing out the book in a record time.

Bijay Kumar Das
Ravenshaw College, Cuttack

Contents

1
Introduction

To make an evaluation of Postmodern Indian English Literature is not an easy task. It raises a number of questions regarding the date and the nature of the subject under discussion. At the outset, I would like to steer clear of all controversies by putting the facts in order. That is, the nomenclature, 'Indian English Literature' has come to stay—thanks to Sahitya Akademi for accepting it and publishing M.K. Naik's seminal book, *A History of Indian English Literature* in 1982. It means the literature originally written in English by Indian nationals including the expatriate Indian writers. The earlier nomenclatures — "Indo-Anglian Literature," "Indian Writing in English," "Indo-English Literature," and "Indian Literature in English"— were dispensed with because of their inadequacies. So, Indian English Literature, like Oriya Literature, Bangla Literature, Tamil Literature, Hindi Literature and so on, is a valid nomenclature and should not be taken as a protean term. Some critics may argue that since Indian English Literature is a part of Post-colonial Literature *(i.e.,* literatures written in English in former British colonies), its identity can be questioned. My answer is that if Oriya literature and Kannada literature could be considered indigenous and independent literatures despite being part of Indian Literature, then why can't we take Indian English Literature as a distinct, independent and indigenous Indian Literature despite it being a part of Post-colonial literature.

The next question is why 'Post-1980' should be a cut off period for Indian English Literature. To my mind, substantial body of Indian English Literature — be it, poetry, fiction, short- story, autobiography and drama — was written in the post-1930 era, notwithstanding the origin of poetry, fiction and short- story in the nineteenth century. It is the great trio — Mulk Raj Anand,

R.K. Narayan and Raja Rao who wrote novel and stories in the nineteen thirties, and Nissim Ezekiel, Kamala Das, A.K. Ramanujan who wrote poetry in the sixties, have greatly contributed to the creation of a new literature in English in our country. Their creative effort got the critical sanction in the hands of critics like K.R.S. Iyengar, C.D. Narasimhaiah and a few others in the nineteen sixties. It is unthinkable to conceive of Indian English literature as a distinct literature without Iyengar's book, *Indian Writing in English*.

We can divide Indian English Literature from 1930s to the end of the 20th century into two phases: Modernist and Postmodernist, the former beginning with Raja Rao's *Kanthapura* (1938) and the latter beginning with Salman Rushdie's *Midnight's Children* (1981) and Nissim Ezekiel's *Latter-Day Psalms* (1982). In the Post-1980 era Indian English literature is marked by postmodernism and can be profitably analysed in terms of Post-colonial theory so assiduously built up by Gareth Griffiths, Bill Ashcroft and Helen Tiffin basing upon Edward Said's *Orientalism,* and *Culture and Imperialism.* Important poets, novelists, short-story writers and playwrights in the post-1980 period include the names of Nissim Ezekiel, A.K. Ramanujan, Jayanta Mahapatra, Kamala Das, Shiv K. Kumar, Keki N. Daruwalla, Dom Moraes, Amitav Ghosh, Shashi Tharoor, Upamanyu Chatterjee, Shashi Deshpande, Anita Desai, Vikram Seth, Vikram Chandra, Arundhati Roy, Manju Kapur, Raj Kamal Jha, Ruskin Bond, Manoj Das, Hari Kunzru and a few others. (I do not include the name of Salman Rushdie in this list, because he is not an Indian English writer, though he is of Indian origin. No doubt, he has inspired Indian English Writers in the eighties and after, and his *Midnight's Children* has acquired the status of a classic. Even then, technically he cannot be considered as an Indian English Writer, because he is not a citizen of our country.)

Indian English Writers in the nineteen eighties and after come under criticism for what the Bhasa literature critics call the lack of authenticity and Indian sensibility in their writings. We sometimes call an Indian English writer, an Indian writer in English. But we never say an Indian writer in Oriya or in Bengali Why? That is, because we consider English an 'alien language,' the language of the Imperialistic power. But we tend to forget that English has been with us for more than two centuries. It has been granted the status of an associate official language of India and what is more, the National Akademi of Letters gives annual awards to Indian English writers along with bhasa writers. English is no less ours, for it is primarily being an Englishman's or an American's language. We have bi-lingual writers who write both in English and in their regional languages. For instance, Manoj Das writes stories in English as well as in Oriya. Similarly Kamala Das writes both in English and in Malayalam. So, one does not become less authentic and a lesser Indian if he writes in English. It is not always true that a writer chooses his language, the language too chooses him. That is, one will write in that language in which he has literary competence. Meenakshi Mukherjee makes a pertinent observation on this point in the following words:

> I cannot imagine any Indian—whether Punjabi, Bengali or Oriya—one day making a deliberate decision to write in English because it would guarantee him a wide audience and ensure access to the literary reproduction system of a world market, hence yield royalties in foreign exchange. Those who write in English do so because—no matter what language they speak at home they have literary competence only in English. Contrary to popular belief, not all of them achieve fame abroad, and it is possible that some are read by numerically fewer people than read a bhasa novel. It may be more useful for us to understand the circumstances that lead to the loss of the mother tongue than to charge these writers for capitalizing on their loss (2000:169).

In recent years *(i.e.,* the post-1980 period) Indian English literature unlike Bhasa literatures (it is a term used by G.N. Devy to mean literatures written in regional Indian languages) is the only pan-Indian literature. It is a literature that has readers all over the country. The writers of Bhasa literatures like Oriya, Bengali, Telugu etc. do not have readers outside the respective language and the language groups. Moreover, Indian English writers get recognition abroad before they gain acceptance at home.

There is another charge against the Indian English Writers—that is, they do not have contact with the 'live language.' But most of these writers in the post-1980 era live almost half of the year either in Britain or in America. They have contact with the 'live language' and have gained inwardness with it. Apart from that, these writers have almost succeeded in creating a new Indian English idiom by taking recourse to code mixing in their work. Indian English fiction writers in particular have succeeded in making Indian English idioms and expressions acceptable to the Anglo-American readers.

Postmodern Indian English literature has come up age. It successfully meets the challenges of the Bhasa literatures at home and Postcolonial literature and Anglo-American Literatures abroad. Indian English Literature has transcended 'the local' and transformed it into global. And that is, the hallmark of good literature. This brings to our mind Eliot's observation made in his essay, 'The Three Provincialities':

> "True literature has something which can be appreciated by intelligent foreigners who have a reading knowledge of the language, and also something which can only be understood by the particular people living in the same place as the author" (Rajnath, 2001:26).

Postmodern Indian English Literature has vindicated Eliot's observation in letter and spirit.

Works Cited

Mukherjee, Meenakshi. *The Perishable Empire.* Calcutta: Oxford University Press, 2000.

Rajnath. Quoted. *Literary Criticism in the New Millennium.* Littcrit. 27: 1-2 (Jan.-Dec. 2001).

2
Postmodern Indian English Poetry

Indian English poetry though owes its origin to Henry Derozio's *Poems* published in 1827, it got "a local habitation and a name" with the publication of Nissim Ezekiel's *A Time to Change* in London in 1952. Between Derozio and Ezekiel, we have only a few Indian English poets such as Kashi Prasad Ghosh, Michael Madhu Sudan Dutt, Aru Dutt, Toru Dutt, Manmohan Ghose, Sri Aurobindo, Harindranath Chattopadhya and Sarojini Naidu. Of these poets only three stand out as significant contributors to poetry—they are, Toru Dutt, Sarojini Naidu and Sri Aurobindo. But these three poets, particularly Toru Dutt and Sarojini Naidu are said to have imitated the English poets and Aurobindo is taken to be more a mystic and a yogi than a poet. We need not take this view seriously and dismiss these poets lock, stock and barrel. It will be objective on our part to say that Toru Dutt, Sarojini Naidu and Sri Aurobindo are our most well-known and substantial poets in the Pre-Independence era.

The whole poetic scenario changed with the advent of our Independence and the establishment of Commonwealth group of nations in the post-1950 period. When Leeds University established a Chair for Commonwealth Literature in 1958 and started imparting it as a course, Indian English Literature became a part of it. Thus, Indian English poetry came to be viewed both as an Indian literature and simultaneously as a part of Commonwealth literature. Nissim Ezekiel became the first modern Indian English poet in the post-Independence period and his book of poems, *A Time to Change* can be said to herald modernism in Indian English poetry. Indian English poetry as a distinct genre emerged in the works of Nissim Ezekiel, Kamala

Das and A.K. Ramanujan in the nineteen sixties. Ezekiel's *The Unfinished Man* 1960, *The Exact Name* 1965, Kamala Das' *Summer in Calcutta* 1965 and A.K. Ramanujan's *Striders* 1966 herald a new era for Indian English poetry. I should hasten to add that P. Lal and his publishing firm Writers' Workshop established in 1958 worked as a catalyst to further the cause of Indian English poetry.

The luxuriant growth of Indian English poetry occurred in mid-seventies with the publication of R. Parthasarathy's ably chosen and edited anthology titled, *Ten Twentieth Century Indian Poets* in 1976. This anthology can be said to have marked the beginning of postmodernism in Indian English poetry. This anthology was quickly followed by individual collection of poems such as Nissim Ezekiel's Hymns in *Darkness* (1976), A.K. Ramanujan's *Selected Poems* (1977), Keki N. Daruwalla's *Crossing of Rivers* (1976), R. Parthasarathy's *Rough Passage* (1976) and Shiv K. Kumar's *Subterfuges* (1977). Indian English poetry won recognition both at home and abroad.

A new phase was dawn upon Indian English poetry in the 1980s and after, when our poets were honoured by the Sahitya Akademi, New Delhi with its Annual Award and gained academic acclaim by being prescribed as a course at several Indian universities and abroad.

Sahitya Akademi, New Delhi has honoured seven Indian English poets with its Annual Award in the Post-1980 period. They are Jayanta Mahapatra for *Relationship* in 1981, Nissim Ezekiel for *Latter-Day Psalms* in 1983, Keki N. Daruwalla for *Keeper of the Dead* in 1984, Kamala Das for *Collected Poems Vol. I* in 1985, Shiv K. Kumar for *Trapfalls in the Sky* in 1987, Dom Moraes for *Serendip* in 1994 and A.K. Ramanujan for *Collected Poems* in 1999. If Salman Rushdie's *Midnight's Children* marks postmodernism in Indian English fiction, the works of these poets mentioned above can be said to embody the characteristics of postmodernism and post-colonialism in the last two decades of the twentieth century. In this chapter an attempt has been made to analyse the poetry of those important post-1980 poets in addition to the above-mentioned poets who have enriched Indian English Literature and made it acceptable to the West.

I begin with Nissim Ezekiel. No discussion of Indian English poetry in the post-colonial era can begin with any poet other than Ezekiel. He is to Indian English poetry, what T.S. Eliot is to English poetry. He has given it a direction, an idiom and a sense of purpose and made it immensely popular both at home and abroad. He published two collections of poems— *Latter-Day Psalms* (1982) and *Collected Poems 1952-88* (1989) in the post-1980 period.

Latter-Day Psalms (1982) carries forward the themes and techniques employed in *Hymns in Darkness* (1976) to their logical conclusion. Ezekiel, the ironist and parodist now becomes a humanistic poet, and his poetry has acquired new dimensions by using Indian English idiom for specific purposes. Here, there is variety-realism, love, philosophy, prayer, advice, and specific use of Indian English idiom. Paradox, irony, and antithesis have a free play in this volume. The result is astounding. And the poet is duly honoured by the Central Sahitya Akademi with its Annual Award for 1983. "Healers," "Hangover," and "Very Indian Poems in Indian English" are highly evocative and enjoyable. They speak to us in our own situation. The poet becomes a prophet, and advises us:

> Know your mantra, meditate
> release your kundalini
> get your shakti awakening
> and float with the spirit
> to your destination.

"The Indian landscape seers my eyes" has yielded place to reality and the poet like a detached observer sees and describes what happens all around us. He highlights the funny aspects of our rituals, and way of life in "Jewish Wedding in Bombay," "Hangover" and "The Patriot." In a mock-seriousness in the manner of Brutus, the poet asks:

> Friends, Romans, Countrymen, I am saying
> (to myself)
> Lend me ears.
> Everything is coming—
> Regeneration, Remuneration, Contraception
> Be patiently, brothers and sisters.

Indian reality has become a favourite subject of the poet for contemplation. Hence, Ezekiel chides us for our folly:

> These are the days of family planning.
> I am not against. We have to change with times.
> Whole world is changing. In India also
> We are keeping up. Our progress is progressing.
> Old values are going, new values are coming.
> Everything is happening with leaps and bounds.

With this Ezekiel changes his themes from conventional to unconventional subjects like poverty, sex and benediction. And new themes create new idioms. The form gives a new look to Ezekiel's poetry in this volume.

Ezekiel is a conscious artist. The centre of poetic interest in him lies in the process of adjustment between the knowledge derived from experience or personal feelings and the knowledge which imposes a pattern. To read his poetry is to watch an actor enacting his comic play in all its facets—love, sex, commitment to life on the stage, it is to know him inside out. He deals with love and sex directly and boldly. Ezekiel stands with W.B. Yeats for 'profane perfection of mankind' in which sense and spirit are fully and harmoniously exploited. He writes:

> This longing is for nakedness:
> Soul naked, body naked...
> And let him understand, that in the working
> of his mind the body takes a hand. ("Nakedness")

Ezekiel considers love and the consummation of it as the spring of life. And therefore, he emphasises fulfilment in love leading to marriage. He says,

> Life can be kept alive
> By contact with the unknown and the strange,
> A feeling for the mystery,
> Of man and woman joined, exhaustion
> At the act, desire for it again. ("To a Certain Lady")

Ezekiel seems to say, 'hail wedded love,' for it brings fulfilment to life. Like D.H. Lawrence, he sees marriage and procreation as a mystery:

> Between the acts of wedded love
> A quieter passion flows,
> Which keeps the nuptial pattern firm

As passion comes and goes,
And in the soil of wedded love
Rears a white rose. ("Marriage Poem")

So strongly does he hold this view that he projects the union of man and woman as a key to our survival in this world. Like T.S. Eliot, he also sees marriage as a process essentially of this world and part of the cycle of time:

Destroying or creating, moving on or standing still,
Always we must be lovers,
Man and wife at work upon the hard
Mass of material which is the world. ("To a Certain Lady")

Ezekiel's poetry is a veritable apotheosis and dramatisation of personality through passion and affirmation. His characters—Miss Pushpa T.S., the Railway Clerk, the Professor, the English teacher, Ganga, the maidservant, Guru, and a host of others symbolize the achievement of personality. They are individuals as well as types. His world is warm, palpable and dynamic, his personages are vividly present and recognisable in terms of 'chief intensity' as the poet himself.

But the poem written between 1983 and 1988 show the decline of Ezekiel's poetic craft. He has lost the fire in him, but the glow is still there. There are some good poems, but triviality has taken over seriousness. "Very Indian Poems in Indian English" compared to poems of this category looks like a caricature. For instance, poems like "Soap" and "The Way in went" have lost the driving force of earlier poems.

In this aspect Ezekiel reminds us of W.B. Yeats whose poetry declined after his *The Tower* and *The Winding Stair* volumes. Similarly Ezekiel's poetry declined after *Hymns in Darkness* and *Latter-Day Psalms* volumes. Again like Yeats, Ezekiel excels in short poems and his growth as a poet is continuous till *Latter-Day Psalms.* Like T.S. Eliot, Ezekiel has brought everyday conversational language into the realms of poetry. He came as a liberating force, technically and encouraged poets to make more of inter-play of past, present and future, than they had done before. He helped to popularise free verse in Indian English poetry. The greatest contribution of Ezekiel as a poet lies in giving a kind of confidence, courage and conviction to his fellow Indian English poets to write poetry in their own way free of Anglo-American influence.

Kamala Das, is the second important Indian English poet to appear on the poetic scene after Ezekiel with the publication of her book of verse, *Summer in Calcutta* (1965) in the postcolonial era. She is also the fourth Indian English poet to win the Sahitya Akademi Award for her book, *Collected Poems Vol. I* in 1985. She has published two volumes of poems— *Collected Poems* Vol. I (1984) and *Only the Soul Knows How to Sing* (1996)— in the post-1980 era. Her imaginative world derives its power to involve the reader from its rich mimetic content while its enduring quality comes from verbal imagery drawn from many sources. Thus, she grapples with ideas and abstractions, images of men and women on several planes, the complex of emotions centering round human activities such as love, sex, companionship and problems relating to her own art. Her feminine sensibility finds its true and fullest expression in her love poems. Indian sensibility is transparent in her poetry and the use of Radha Krishna myth makes it more appealing to the Indian readers. Krishna, the eternal lover is a living consciousness among Indians and the epitome of love. The utterance of His name brings joy to millions of people in India. In a poem called 'Ghanashyam,' Kamala Das invokes Lord Krishna with a heart filled with devotion and joy.

A poet may assume an identity by referring to national myths, so that when the myths are employed, the link is immediately established in the minds of the people. The use of national myths helps to create an identity for the poet. Postcolonial poets in their effort to create an identity of their own by way of resisting and subverting the colonizer, make use of national myths. Kamala Das has exactly done that by evoking Mira Bai myth in her poetry. The sudden disappearance of Mira, a devotee of Lord Krishna has become a living myth and legend in our country. Like Mira all devoted and religious minded women desire to merge with the ultimate consciousness—*i.e.,* Lord Krishna. In a poem titled, 'Radha' a virgin girl after the first embrace says crying: 'Everything in me/Is melting, even the hardness at the core/O Krishna, I am melting, melting, melting.' In another poem, 'Krishna' the protagonist surrenders with the following words:

> Your body is my prison, Krishna,
> I cannot see beyond it,

Your darkness blinds me.
Your love words shut out the wide world's din.

In her poetry, apart from love, Kamala Das describes a world which is harsh, sun-pierced tropical world full of smells of rotten garbage and death, where men have 'limbs like carnivorous plants.' The lanes are 'fevered,' the trees dusty and leafless, cheeks 'sub-stained,' only the marigolds and bougainvillea survive, like courtesans with 'tinsel and jasmine in the hair.' The poet herself feels "a hunger to take in with greed, like a forest fire/ that consumes."

In an introduction to Kamala Das' latest volume of poems, *Only the Soul Knows How to Sing,* K. Satchidanandan makes an apt comment in the following lines:

> Old age, death and nothingness are a recurring presence in Kamala's more recent poems. She realises that "at my age there are no longer any home comings" ("Woman's Shuttles"). In "A Cask of Nothing" she says: "If I close my eyes, I see nothing/If I shut my ears I hear nothing. Nothing but nothing/inside or outside/the nothing that resides/as an ache within/the only content/the human cask can contain." In the summer of 1980 she hears only the cry "kill, kill," "Perhaps the malevolent/ Alchemy of the city air/Aided us, turning gold to/ Lead, so that the familiar/Caressing hands unshaped the clay/ And swiftly formed a death-head..." (Summer 1980). She finds a sudden drought to have settled itself down on the "Sun-bleached estuaries" of her blood and wonders whether she is living or dying; all her gestures seem to have a little of each. Death according to her, is the obscure parallel of life (Life's Obscure Parallel). She would go in silence "leaving not even a fingerprint on this crowded earth," carrying away her "bird-in-flight voice" and the "hundred misunderstandings" that ruined her alliances (Death is so Mediocre). Growth, she discovers, is "the stoicism of the sewers/beneath great cities, accepting the rush/ of putrid waste" (1997: 17).

Even when Kamala Das becomes conscious of death, the inevitable, she has not abandoned life nor her sense of longing to belong. Thus, she writes:

Ultimately, we come to know
that for us there is only one

claimant whom by mistake we call
death, obsessed as we are by our
physicality, restrained
by the eyes' inadequate power
to perceive beyond the farthest
precincts of truth. If only he
human eye could look beyond the
chilling flesh, the funeral pyre's
rapid repast and then beyond
the mourner's vanquished stance, where would
death be then, that meaningless word
when life is all that there is, that
raging continuity that
often the wise once recognize as God?

("Anamalai Poems IV" 1997: 109)

If Ezekiel thinks that 'home is where we have to gather grace,' Kamala Das says that 'home is what we return to battered by work/illness or love/home is where the dream awaits us' ('The word is sin'). And again like Ezekiel, Kamala Das brought everyday conversational language into the realms of poetry. There is a free flow of colloquial idiom in her poetry and words as it were, obey her call. Like A.K. Ramanujan, Kamala Das excels in her family poems. If she has glorified grandmother in her earlier poems, in her latest collection she has portrayed her low hate relationship with her father. The three poems about her father — "A Requiem for my Father," "My Father's Death" and "Next to Indira Gandhi" reveals her greatness as a poet. Let us, examine the following extracts:

You were laid out on the drawing room floor,
A dead Nayar gets only the cold floor to lie on.
We remembered your fear of the cold
And your aching spinal bone.
We were sick and cold within.
I would have gladly changed places with you, father.
I was never afraid to die,
From childhood to middle years I have had a raw deal
Illness, and loneliness, loves that faded like mist,
And the elders' irrational hate.
You loved life. ("A Requiem for My Father")

He was generous with money

As generous as I was with
Love. There was a cloud of tension
Between him and me. I brought him
Shame, they say. He brought me on each
Short visit some banana chips
And harsh words of reproach. I feared
My father. Only in a coma
Did he seem close to me, and I
Whispered into his ears that I
Loved him although I was bad, a bad
Daughter, a writer of tales that
Hurt, but in the task of loving
The bad ones were the ablest, yes,
You should have hugged me, father, just
Once, held me to your breast, you should
Have asked me who I was, in truth.

("My Father's Death")

Father, I ask you now without fear
Did you want me
Did you ever want a daughter
Did I disappoint you much
With my skin as dark as yours...
You chose my clothes for me
My tutors, my hobbies, my friends,
And at fifteen with my first saree you picked me a husband
I am grateful
For choosing for me a man
And a life of suburban dullness
Brightened with embroidery and crochet work
And the Thursday Cookery class
But it was not the rightmost groove for me
It wasn't my cup of tea
I know I let you down, father.
But you have punished me enough, haven't you?

("Next to Indira Gandhi")

The autobiographical note is unmistakable. The sincerity of emotions and feelings, the agony and the anguish go together in these poems. The empirical personality and the implied personality become one and what is more, here the love triumphs over hate. Both in content and in form, Kamala Das poetry shows originality and reveals Indian sensibility. Above all, her poetry contributes substantially to the creation of an Indian English idiom that helps us to distinguish Indian English poetry from poetry written in English anywhere in the world.

A.K. Ramanujan is one of the most significant Indian English poets, who together with Ezekiel and Kamala Das, gave an identity and a sense of direction to Indian English poetry in the nineteen sixties. He has published two volumes of poems, *Second Sight* (1986) and *The Collected Poems of A.K. Ramanujan* (incorporating *The Black Hen*) (1995) in the post-1980 era. Family remains one of his major themes in these two volumes and that in a Way establishes link with his earlier poetry. In 'Extended Family,' the poet recalls his grandfather on the one hand and imagines his great-great-grandson and takes a vow not to be 'dependent/on several people/yet to come.' In "Love Poem for a Wife and Her Trees" Ramanujan imaginatively perceives three generation of women—Mother/wife and daughter in linear progression. His family has its 'roots in heaven/and branches in the earth.' In another poem called, 'Looking for the Centre' Ramanujan tries to discover his roots and finding it not easy, he tries to extricate himself from this bondage. Thus, he says,

> Suddenly, connections severed
> as in a lobotomy, unburdened
> of history, I lose
> my bearings, a circum Zilla Spun
> at the end of her rope, dizzy
> terrified.
> and happy...

Behind the search for family connections there lies the groundswell for diving deep in order to discover the roots. The country of his birth haunts his mind without end. Thus, the poet says,

> As I transact with the past as with another
> Country with its own customs, currency,
> stock exchange, always at a loss when
> I count my change: ('Waterfalls in a Bank')

Ramanujan wants to put all his experiences and visions into the texture of his poetry. Like Eliot who says in his *The Waste Land,* 'I can connect nothing with nothing.' Ramanujan wants to do the same thing though in a limited way. In a poem entitled 'Connect,' Ramanujan clearly states:

Connect! Connect—Cries my disconnecting
madness, resembling phrases.
See the Cycles.
father whispers in my ear, black holes and
white noise, elections with four-year shadows, red eclipses
and the statistics of rape. Connect,
Connect, beasts with monks, slave economies
and the golden bough.

Hindu consciousness is pivotal to Ramanujan's thinking. It is this consciousness which binds him to his tradition though he lives in a different country now. The title poem of the *Second Sight* states this unambiguously:

"You are a Hindoo, aren't you?
You must have Second Sight." ('Second Sight')

Ramanujan combines his scholarship with poetic insight and the result is astounding. Like T.S. Eliot, Ramanujan is a very learned poet and his learning his proverbial. Besides being a Professor of Linguistics with a very wide range of learning, he is a folklorist. "No Fifth Man," a poem included in *The Black Hen* tells us about the story of five brahmans who went abroad to study all the sixty-four arts, wanted to show off their knowledge by bringing a dead tiger back to life and in the process all but one lost their lives. The fifth one who had commonsense was saved. Ramanujan puts the whole story in its proper perspective.

The fifth man, the coward
cried, "wait, wait
just one second"
and climbed up a tree in a hurry
while the fourth chanted a mantra
gave the tigress life...
and the creature pounced on him
his three friends rooted
in their fear, killed them all
and ate them up for starters
Nothing was left of them
not even a bone. (*CP* 244-45)

In "Mythologies 1," Ramanujan describes the Purana myth (the demon who offered her poisoned breast to Lord Krishna to suck from, in which the demon got a new life in her death). The paradox is that by getting killed in the act of offering poisoned milk to the Lord, she got deliverance from the life of a demon. Thus, he writes:

The Child took her breast
in his mouth and sucked it right out of her chest
Her carcass stretched from North to South
She changed, undone by grace
from deadly mother to happy demon
found life in death. (*CP* 221)

In "Mythologies *2*" Ramanujan shows how Lord Vishnu kills a person, howsoever, clever who has got a boon not to be killed:

When the clever man asks the perfect boon:
not to be slain by demon, God, or by
beast, not by day or by night,
by no manufactured weapon, not out
Of doors nor inside, not in the sky
nor on earth,
Come now come soon,
Vishnu, man, lion, neither and both, to hold
him in your lap to disembowel his pride
with the steel glint of bare claws at twilight. (*CP*226)

Ramanujan's knowledge of Indian myths and folklore is amazing. And he makes use of myths and folklore as themes in his poetry. And it is in this aspect that his poetry conforms to the norm of post-colonial literature.

Ramanujan's poetry closely monitors the relation between nature and the human body and examines the impact of culture and time on this relationship. The interactions of body with the natural world are skillfully worked out in poems like "Love Poem for a Wife and Her Trees" and "Looking for the Centre." Ramanujan maintains that physical reproduction occurs in the branches of 'family trees,' 'with their roots in heaven/ and branches in the earth.' He metaphorically says that an "anatomy of text-book" which unfolds 'a human body, layer/underlayer, skin, muscle, ganglia/of nerves, branching red' is finally put 'into a map of the heavens,' meaning man is inextricably bound to the cosmos. In the significant poem called "One More on a Deathless Theme" included in *The Black Hen* Ramanujan further works out on the theme of 'the body-nature nexus.' The body after death returns to nature. As the poet says:

> Everyone in this street
> will become cold, lie under stones
> or be scattered as ash
> in rivers and oceans. (*CP* 210)

Apart from bringing a correlation between 'body' and 'nature' in his poetry, Ramanujan also points out that 'time and culture form an integral part of human life.' As he puts it:

> Time moves in and out of me
> a stream of sound, a breeze,
> an electric current that seeks
> the ground, ...
> Morning brown
> into evenings before I turn around
> in the day. (Sonnet *CP* 220)

Ramanujan like Eliot does not believe that time is linear. It is the cyclic process of life that rotates forever.

It is often argued that there are two ways of writing poetry: One, basing upon inspiration *(i.e.,* spontaneously) and two, making an effort for it. Though good poetry is written in both ways, Ramanujan believes in the second method. Reversing Keats' dictum Ramanujan tells us that a poem comes not always as leaves to a tree, but differently. One has to work on it. Taking black hen as a metaphor for a poem, he says:

> It must come as leaves
> to a tree
> or not at all
> Yet it comes sometimes
> as the black hen
> with the red round eye
> on the embroidery
> stitch by stitch
> dropped and found again
> and when it's all there
> the black hen stares
> with its round eye
> and you're afraid. (The Black Hen, *CP* 195)

As stated in "Poetry and Our City," Ramanujan while writing poetry 'settles down to free verse.' Not only that, 'irony' becomes a favourite mode in his poetry, like Ezekiel's 'Guru' who is scrupulous in checking the accounts of the Ashram, Ramanujan's 'Guru' exploits the disciple and is hypocritical by nature. The 'Guru' in the poem, "The Guru" asked his disciple not to do certain things. Disregarding his advice the protagonist did otherwise:

> I gave the dog his bone, the parrot
> his seed, the pet snake his mouse
> forgave the weasel his tooth
> forgave the tiger his claw
> and left the guru to clean his shoe
> for I remembered I was born of a woman. (*CP* 251)

Ramanujan's poetry is 'worldly' (to use a term of Edward Said) and it is always an affirmation of life as stated in the following lines:

> Yet days can be golden, apples beautiful,
> if eyes can see only days and apples. ("If Eyes can see")

Jayanta Mahapatra who like Keki N. Daruwalla and Shiv K. Kumar appeared on the map of Indian English poetry in nineteen seventies has two things to his credit. One, he is the first ever Indian English poet to win Sahitya Akademi Award for his book of verse, *Relationship* in 1981 and second, he is the most prolific Indian English poet with sixteen volumes of poetry to his credit. In the post-1980 era he has published ten volumes of poetry surpassing all Indian English poets and earned a name as India's foremost poet writing in English language. His magnum opus *Relationship* combines the three: history, myth and vision. It is set in a land of 'forbidding myth'—*i.e.* Orissa. Jayanta Mahapatra does the same thing in *Relationship* as R. Parthasarathy did in *Rough Passage* in trying to acclimatize English language to an indigenous tradition. The myth of twelve hundred artisans working day and night to complete the Konarka temple under the authority of a "ruthless emperor" has evoked sympathy in our hearts. From the building of Konarka temple Mahapatra takes us down the memory lane to our "maritime ancestors" who brought glory to the State. Time has withered away everything, but the racial memory haunts the poet without end. The Mahanadi, Konarka and 'maritime' ancestors remind the poet of a glorious past of the land of his birth and thus, he ends the first section of *Relationship* with a sense of belonging:

> Only that the stones were my own,
> waiting as mother or goddess or witch,
> as my birth feeds on them
> as though the empty dugs of sorcerous thought.

The heroic past is vividly remembered and recalled with great despair. The 'guilt consciousness' haunts him without end when the realisation is drawn upon him that his generation has not been able to keep up the martial tradition of his ancestors. The glory and pride of our ancestors exhibited in the climatic Kalinga war in 261 B.C. which changed the Emperor Ashok, the Great from a despotic monarch to a deeply religious man are things of the past. The river Daya is a silent witness to our ancestors' heroic act all through the ages. Thus, the poet writes:

> Orion crawls like a spider in the sky
> while the swords of forgotten kings
> rust slowly in the museum of our guilt.

The poet is at a loss to understand how the successors of such great ancestors have become so unheroic and unworthy of their predecessors. An awareness of contemporary situation brings the poet to the realm of history of our land right from the time Lord Buddha sat in meditation 'under the *peepal* tree.' Then he traces his own birth at Cuttack where numerous gods and goddesses are worshipped, a city of historical importance which had the great Barabati Fort/is now a symbol of 'vanquished dynasties.' The past is brought alive for a moment, 'of broken empires and of vanquished dynasties,/and of ahimsa whimpers.' The poet now standing among the ruin's drifts through his weariness, listening to the voices of his friends and 'writing poems,' 'with the smells of the rancid fat of the past.'

Mahapatra's pre-occupation with the naked earth of which Orissa forms a significant part—the favourite places such as Jagannath Puri, Cuttack, Bhubaneswar dominates his thought and helps him to search for his 'self.' There is, as it were, a total identification of the man with his environment, the earth that raised him and this approach brings Mahapatra closer to leading Commonwealth poets.

To my mind *Relationship* is a very successful poem that reveals an Indian sensibility and, in a way, creates an Indian English idiom. The poem is set in Orissa and the history and myth of Mahapatra's land of birth are built into the texture of this poem. It at once gives a kind of identity to Indian English poetry by acclimatizing an indigenous tradition to English language.

The first section of the poem though overworked with images succeeds in conveying the impossibility of unravelling the mystery of life. The heroic past of the land of Orissa has been revoked with a sense of pride.

> Time
> and the boat,
> and the initiation into the mystery of peace,
> the sailing ships of those maritime ancestors,
> who have vanished in the black Bay without a trace,
> that only live in the sound of the waves
> flinging themselves into the dark fringes
> of this land from Chilika to Chandipur. (*Relationship* 1)

The first section of the poem serves as an exposition when references are made to the Mahanadi, the prime river of the State, the temple of Konarka, the ancient harbours like Chilika and Chandipur. There is search for roots and the heroic Oriya past is vividly remembered and recalled with a sense of nostalgia. The glory and pride of our ancestors exhibited in the climatic Kalinga War in 261 B.C. which turned Ashok, the Great into a deeply religious man is now a long-lost trait in our racial character and behaviour. The river Daya is a witness to our ancestor's heroic effort which has become a sort of myth for us. Once heroic and militant race is now no more than a mere memory now for its successors proved to be unworthy of keeping the glory of their ancestors afloat and drifted away from their ideals. Thus, the poet begins with a sense of dispossession and gradually moves towards rootedness—leading from guilty, deprivation and hurtful otherness to a joyful sense of being re-united with one's origin and source.

Bare Face (2000) reiterates Mahapatra's commitment as a post-colonial poet. For example, 'A Pastoral Perhaps' reveals his concern for national identity. The opening stanza of the poem depicts a village scene (India lives in her villages, said Gandhiji and rightly so) which is evocative of the spirit of true India.

By the scummy pond, in the thin rain,
a woman shakes her hair loose,
before entering the water. Through the grove
of bamboos dripping bright raindrops,
a long-abandoned thought appears to push a smile
at her lips. Audacious shadows open
to take her in; she shrugs, strong unaware.

The image of a village woman entering into a pond, shaking her hair loose to have her bathe and the raindrops dripping through the bamboo grove, brings the rural India alive in the minds of the readers. The second stanza reinforces the idea of true India lying in her villages, when the landscape of the place is integrated with history of the country—the past is dovetailed into the present and merges with it. Mahapatra writes:

Leaves green, sway under the cloudy sky
and only the woman's sun bronzed face looks out
above the water. The air drops quietly back into the past
a part of the present seems to break away.
The destiny of India heaves in darkness,
in the memory of ancient waters.

The history of India is now in the pond where the woman bathes, it is in a way, re-locating the past in the present, a preoccupation of post-colonial writers (poets included). This is what Eliot did in a grand way in 'Little Gidding' *(Four Quartets).*

Mahapatra tries to bring an integration between landscape and people in a poem called "In a Time of Winter Rain" and tells us how the evocative memory of the past recreates the present. Thus, he writes:

We learn to smile in a time of winter rain.
Under a wet sky it's no meagre comfort
to feel the radiance of noon in our palms
the almond-eyed boats clutching time in their fists
in the Mahanadi River, the right shoulders
of peaceful lotuses floating motionless.
How I have waited, shaped by memory!
these many years without knowing exactly why
Does childhood spread out all the way
from the hills of innocence to the horizon of the sea?

Mahapatra has made an effort to evoke a typical Indian atmosphere by describing the Indian sky, landscape, birds and even abandoned temples in his poetry. In our country sometimes some temples are abandoned, and rituals are not performed. Then, in some cases the worship resumes after sometime. Jayanta Mahapatra describes an abandoned temple in a poem called, "Abandoned Temple," and thereby re-creates an actual scene in the following lines:

A wandering boy hurls a rock through
the ruined entrance. Shadows in retreat fly:
the serpent-girls, elephant-gods, fiery birds.
Mosquitoes slap the Siva *linga* in ignorant stillness
a long shiver running down the shrine.

The attempt to build a lively atmosphere out of the surroundings and evoke a sense of 'nativism' is part of the strategy of post-colonial writings. The post-colonial writers seek to describe the indigenous culture and thereby assert their nationality that is both lovable and enduring.

Not only that, like Raja Rao in Indian English fiction (in *Kanthapura,* to be precise), Mahapatra also tries to create a contemporary myth out of Gandhi in his recent poetry. Gandhi has become a living myth suggesting non-violence, truth and righteousness. Furthermore, Gandhi has also become a synonym for justice and honesty, and passed into Indian mind as an apostle of peace. To deify Gandhi, is part of the process of decolonising the Indian mind and hence, Gandhi becomes an integral part *(i.e.,* a major subject) of post-colonial literature. Mahapatra's "Requiem" (A poem on Gandhi) is a case in point. Section XII begins with a statement:

You became the red earth
that a perfect, constant gravity
achieved through the aeons.

and closes with the glorification of 'ahimsa,' Gandhi's principled approach to protest against the unjust persons and injustice in the colonial era, under the British Imperialism.

It is a world in itself
this ahimsa,
with its mysterious shadows
lurking under ancient places,

that assumes the clear, self-sustaining light of suns:
a redefinition of beauty

While trying to mythicize Gandhi, Mahapatra realises that one can be authentic as a writer or poet by going back to his/her root. In his case, he wants to decolonise himself and his culture so that he can be original and authentic, as a poet. In trying 'to be himself,' he found his poetry. Thus, he writes:

And the poem I found at last,
already lost in the small of the heart,
just to push the deep, nameless breath
into the hysterics of history. (Section XVIII)

Gandhi has become a living legend for us. Even when people disagree with him or with his principles, they are conscious of his presence. He has become a part of Indian Psyche. In a fitting tribute to Gandhi the poet acknowledges Gandhi's unseen presence amongst us, the Indians. Thus, he writes:

In me
your body opens slowly
as if you have been bound tight all your life,
as if flesh could see
what the mind believes is true. (Section XIX)

The poet comes down heavily on those who wrongly criticise Gandhi and pay only lip service to him. He says,

Today the voice that points a finger at you
floats over the breath of discarded ideas,
the breath of dead flowers day after day at Raj Ghat
(Section XIX)

And for these misguided people Gandhi has become a faded picture. With a tinge of irony, Mahapatra writes:

What you have left behind are
faded pictures on bare office walls. A day
every year as a national holiday. (Section XX)

If creating new national myths is part of Post-colonial writing, Jayanta Mahapatra can truly be called a Post-colonial poet.

Shiv K. Kumar (1921-) has published seven volumes of poems and the eighth is in the pipeline. He owns Sahitya Akademi Award for his fifth book of verse, *Trapfalls in the Sky* in 1987. His three post-1980 collections of poems include *Trapfalls in the Sky* (1986), *Woolgathering* (1998), *Thus Spake the Buddha*

(2001) and the eighth collection of poems *Losing My Way* will appear in 2003.

In Trapfalls in the Sky Kumar gives a distinct touch to Indian sensibility. The book is divided into three sections: "On Native Grounds," "Under Alien Skies," and "Genesis." Here, Kumar tries to assimilate the Eastern and the Western Values of life with a sense of detachment and objectivity. A poem titled, 'An Indian Mother's Advice to her Daughter before Marriage' is a typical example of how Indian mothers tender advice to their daughters to get in on in married life.

> A man's memory is myopic
> like a sparrow's, once filled up
> he hardens into a bedrock.
> And often, at night you may find
> yourself alone, pulling feathers
> out of your pillow. But he patient.
> If he's gone out fishing down the dark
> river he'll be back
> for in spite of his appetite, a man
> cannot swallow both ends of the rainbow.

Like Ezekiel, Kumar is against mechanical performance of rituals. He is in favour of the subversion of tradition and rituals and, therefore, irony becomes a favourite mode in his poetry. Instead of river Ganga cleansing us, we need to cleanse it to get rid of water pollution. Thus, he writes:

> It's only when they are carried down the river of time
> that iron sinks into their souls.
> The waters then get sullied by ritual and dogma-
> ashes and bones,
> wilted floral offerings to be dead,
> and the noontime sweat oozing from the saffron-
> striped for heads of the crocodiles
> whose yawning jaws chant mantras in some obsolete
> tongue.
> May be if someone could dismantle all scaffoldings
> along the mother river's waistline
> and ask the dead to seek immersion
> in other confluences,
> the little fish will then bleach these waters
> for the sun's lasers to probe her limpid groin.
>
> ("Cleansing Ganga")

As a post-colonial poet, Kumar makes an attempt to come to terms with contemporary reality. The picture of the capital city of India *(i.e.,* Delhi) is brought alive in a poem called "O Delhi." To read the poem is to know 'the horror and boredom' of life in this city and it is to see it inside out. Kumar recalls his harrowing days when he landed in Delhi as a refugee. In a "frigid morning," Kumar landed in Delhi, which received him with open arms.

> ...I felt redeemed
> as you threw open your gates—Kashmir and Ajmeri—
> to welcome indoors a fugitive from another land.
> I savoured your hospitality.

But this Delhi is no more. The poet, who like Adam inherited 'a new garden' asks Delhi: 'What have you done to yourself?' And then makes a prophesy:

> I prophesy that you too will fall
> like Nineveh and Babylon
> and no new Indraprastha will rise
> from your barren ashes.

Kumar's treatment of the theme of love in terms of the elements of Indian landscape has the poetic reconciliation of the spirit and the country. He incorporates the heat and dust, the sun and flood, the crowd, the sense of poverty and deprivation into the texture of his moods. Images of 'India' are handled with a consummate skill and keenness of intellect in Kumar's poetry. Unlike other post-colonial Indian English poets Kumar writes a number of poems on the West and sees it from the Indian viewpoint. His poetry fits into the definition of postcolonial literature which states that the post-colonial writer writes back (the empire writes back). Two sections of *Trapfalls in the Sky* ('Under Alien Skies' and 'Genesis') are about the West. Kumar's poetry exhibits both 'subversion' and 'resistance'—the two important traits of post-colonial literature.

Kumar's sixth book of poems, *Woolgathering* marks the culmination of all his earlier books of verse and is a remarkable achievement. Here, Kumar gives vent to his memory and desire and makes an assertion of 'self through dream and reality. Life, love, and death—three eternal themes of poetry are worked out artistically in this volume. The poet has come to terms with the mystery of life and declares in 'On Listening to Mozart's Requiem':

I know when the wind waves its wand,
it's time to give up.

The world of human beings is contrasted with the world of birds in the manner of Keats', poem "Ode to a Nightingale," in "Talking to a Bird on my Window-sill," to bring home the agony of life. 'People may change and smile, but the agony abides,' Kumar seems to say. Thus, he writes:

You seem to chirp your way through life—
never a streak of sorrow in your beady eyes.
You don't know the problems I have to face—
darkness, rain, nightmares—
or that cyclone, last summer, that uprooted
a tree in my compound, demolishing
a nest that had sheltered my vagrant thoughts.

Kumar's poetry being image oriented, it falls into the category of 'Oblique Poetry,' in contrast with 'Direct Poetry' which yields meaning at the surface level. Kumar's poetry makes sense at the deep level, and therefore, irony becomes an important mode in his poetry. For example, an unhappy marriage and divorce are skillfully worked out through subtle imagery and irony in a poem called, "I Say it on Oath, Your Lordship." As Kumar puts it:

I say it on oath, your Lordship,
that I'll speak the truth
and nothing but the truth.
....
Speaking out one's mind in an open court
is always an embarrassment
like the wedding-kiss
under the priest's direction.
So may I use my own language, please
which speaks more through vehicle
than tenor?
I was always subjected to the terrors
of her scimitar-tongue, which hurt me
like a surgeon, doing the stitches
without anaesthesia.
....
Your Lordship,
how I have withstood these assaults
on my mind's fragile fortress

But now I pray that this siege be lifted....
No more, Your Lordship—
I close my evidence.

Poems on Indian landscape are integrated with the contemporary life in our society as in "Banaras: Winter Morning," "Dawn break over Khasi Hills," "Musings in a Park," and "Moongazing." Kumar is successful in evoking contemporary reality in his poetry. He has an eye for details and nothing untoward escapes his notice—be it the priest who 'chants louder/for a generous tip' as in "Crematorium at Adikmet, Hyderabad" or the darkness which 'has its own norms' as in "Blackout" (like Ezekiel's darkness which has many secrets that light does not know). Apart from the world, death has also attracted the attention of the poet and he wrote some of the poems on this theme in *Woolgathering*. He has written about the elusive nature of writing poetry and the secrets of sorrow in married life in poems like "To a Young Beautiful Woman Aspiring to be a Poet" and "Twenty-fifth Wedding Anniversary" respectively. He says,

In any case, writing a poem is like breaking
a genie into doing a tantric ritual
Even the Sphinx was struck dumb, not knowing
how to solve the riddle
of clipping the wings
of a wanton smile.

('To a Young Beautiful Woman
Aspiring to be a Poet')

There's the first knock at the door—
they have started to pour in,
each wearing his own anniversary on his painted face
poised to wish us many returns of the day—
or the night of eternal discord?

('Twenty-fifth Wedding Anniversary')

But Kumar is not a pessimist poet. He has not abandoned hope. He does not believe that an affair can destroy the virtue of a man. Thus, he questions:

How could virtue be sullied
by a night's brief affair? ('The Ring')

His seventh book of verse, *Thus Spake the Buddha* contains 41 poems on a wide variety of subjects ranging from personal loss to impersonal and objective observation of contemporary life and situation. The poet has come to terms with his old age and turned philosophical. He has moved from the possessiveness in life to the renunciation of it. He seeks redemption in life and his later poetry is burdened with the consciousness of regaining innocence in life. Two poems, "Lord Krishna to Arjuna," and "Renunciation," stand out in this volume as an epitome of Kumar's spiritual consciousness. Kumar's "Lord Krishna to Arjuna," reminds us of Eliot's "Dry Salvages" (the third poem in *Four Quartets*), and is imbued with wisdom that human beings wish to acquire in life. When Arjun links the thought of the action with the consequence, Lord Krishna dispels his ignorance. Kumar gives a brilliant exposition of this theme in the following lines:

> O Lord.
> Can an act be divorced from the thought
> of recompense?
> That's man's ultimate frailty, O Warrior,
> to know what lies beyond the horizon,
> to know the end even before the beginning,
> to know if the seed would spout
> into a leaf, and the leaf into a bud—
> if a traveller would reach his destination
> before sunset. No, you'd never know
> what lies ahead because I hold this card
> close to my chest. Or, to put it differently,
> it lies in a sealed capsule, under the ocean's
> bed, inaccessible to man. Though I know it all,
> for I do the choosing—the epicentre
> of the next quake, the point of shipwreck
> on the ocean's surface, or the arrow
> that would transfix the fish's eye in a water bowl.
> I choose the sex in the womb,
> the hurricane's direction and velocity.
> If man were to know his future,
> wouldn't he plays God?

The fact is that, as Eliot puts it in 'Dry Salvages,' "For us there is only the trying/the rest is not our business." Kumar makes it plain when he says, "Act in the present, banishing all thoughts of the future." Kumar realises the ultimate truth of life by accepting fate that is irrevocable. So he says (Lord Krishna's words to Arjuna):

Then pick up your bow and arrow, O Warrior,
and fight to set the crooked straight.
Your destiny was etched on your palm
at birth. Just as it was preordained
that I accompany you, like the musk
in a deer's navel—a whisper in the air
that leads a lone traveller through a wilderness.
May be I took the human form solely to commune
with you, as we both find ourselves here
between the two forces, good and evil.
A mentor too realizes himself
through his disciple, like the Creator
seeing his image in his creation.

The last poem 'Renunciation' is the logical conclusion of the truth that has been drawn upon the poet in the previous poem. Pain is inseparable from life. Thus, he writes:

Pain, he has now learnt, is born
in the mother's womb, and ends only
when the ashes are silenced—
by a sprinkling of milk.
This happened, more than two millennia ago
when sages lived in cages, in harmony
with the wind, rain, thunder—
and the beasts.

With this Kumar has acquired the wisdom of humility and humility is endless.

Kumar deals with national and transnational themes with an open mind. Poverty, superstition, injustice, hypocrisy double-dealing, failure in married life, and betrayal in life in the contemporary society—all come within the purview of his poetry. Sufferings in personal life and sufferings in the society at large make him sad and he exposes those who are responsible for the sufferings of the common people. As he concentrates on contemporary situation, he shuns the use of myths in his poetry. He does not glorify the tradition, on the other hand, he lays emphasis on contemporary reality. The whole country (*i.e.*, the whole of India) becomes the locale of his poetry—a priest of Varanasi, a crematorium at Hyderabad, the pavement sleepers in Bombay, a temple in Calcutta, women at the village wells anywhere in the country and the death of a foreign missionary in Orissa etc—come within the purview of his searching eye and he writes animatedly about them. Kumar depicts the sad incident of an Australian Missionary, Graham Staines' death in a poem titled 'Murder of a Missionary' in a tone imbued with pathos. The humanist in Kumar is clearly seen in the following lines:

> Sundown. A van carrying him and his two sons
> is torched. A frantic struggle to escape
> but they're speared back into the inferno.
> An anguished sky blazes a forked lightning
> to signal the end of innocence.
> ....
> when the media flashed his photograph,
> he looked like a prophet who'd walked
> over the Pacific waters, all the way
> from his land of Kangaroo, to seek
> crucifixion far away from home.

This poem can also be taken as an example of Kumar's transnationalism in which he laments the death of a foreigner and his two sons in our country.

Like Ramanujan here, and Eliot, there, Kumar is a very learned poet. His vast learning and scholarship of English literature—particularly that of Shakespeare and Eliot go a long way to build a poetic style of his own. The echoes of Shakespeare and Eliot are heard frequently. Take for example, his poem 'Birth of my Son,' where he writes:

> In the beginning was the cry
> not the word. But didn't it sound
> like a loud protest against what was to follow?

This reminds us of Shakespeare's words, "When we are born, we cry because we have come to a great stage of fools." Paradoxical statements and anti-thesis abound in Kumar's Poetry as in Eliot's *Four Quartets*. References to *Bhagabat Gita* in a poem called "Lord Krishna to Arjuna" is reminiscent of Eliot's *Four Quartets*. Kumar also echoes some of Nissim Ezekiel's ideas and employs his strategies in quite a few of his poems. Shakespeare's 'the lunatic—the lover and the poet,' Ezekiel's "the poet—the lover and the bird watcher" seem to have influenced Kumar to create a syndrome like, 'the lover, the cancer—patient and the petitioner' in "Tis Hazari Courts, Delhi." This is not to suggest that Kumar is an inferior poet. Chaucer, Shakespeare, Eliot—all have borrowed ideas and imagery from several sources. It is not important what a poet borrows but what he does with his borrowings. Chaucer, Shakespeare, Eliot all have borrowed skeletons from several sources, but they have injected flesh and blood into their borrowings. As a result, their poetry became lively, vigorous and enjoyable, so is the case with Shiv K. Kumar. Kumar being a Professor of English brings all his knowledge of English literature and literatures in English (including American Literature) into the realms of his poetry. Thus, his poetry becomes vibrant and enjoyable. Is not it Eliot who said, "Immature poets imitate, mature poets steal?" Kumar's poetry with its innovative imagery and learned vocabulary may appear difficult at the surface level but as one dives deep into the deep structure, the hard shell of the coconut gets ruptured, the sweet kernel emerges and satisfies the quench of the reader.

Keki N. Daruwalla is the third Indian English poet after Mahapatra and Ezekiel to win the Sahitya Akademi Award for his book of verse, *The Keeper of the Dead* in 1984. Like Mahapatra and Kumar, he appeared on the Indian English poetic scene in the seventies, and has eight collections of poems to his credit. His post-1980 volumes include *Winter Poems* (1980), *The Keeper of the Dead* (1982), *Landscapes* (1987), *A Summer of Tigers* (1995) and *Night River* (2000). He has successfully evoked the Indian landscape in his poetry and availed himself of contemporary reality to such an extent that he ranks among the front ranking post-colonial Indian English poets like Nissim Ezekiel, A.K. Ramanujan, R. Parthasarathy, Jayanta Mahapatra and a few others. In his introduction to *Two Decades of Indian Poetry* 1960-80, Daruwalla writes:

> My poems are rooted in landscape which anchors the poem. The landscape is not merely there to set the scene but to lead to an illumination. It should be the eye of the spiral. I try that poetry, relate to the landscape, both on the physical and on the plane of the spirit. For me riot-stricken town is landscape (1980: 21).

The landscape has a deep impact on life and it is integrated with seasons. No wonder, that it has great influence over the lovers. In a poem titled "From the Snows in Ranikhet" (To a friend newly married). Daruwalla writes:

It's pleasant thought that seasons
will in each other blend
while you move along a landscape
of yearning that will end
in the precincts of your bodies
which you'll seed and tear and rent.

Large-scale deaths in India because of disease and lack of medical facilities upset the poet and he writes a lot of poems on this theme in *The Keeper of the Dead.* Death is the central metaphor in this volume. Daruwalla as it were, "was much possessed by death/And saw skull beneath the skin." In 'Pestilence in Nineteenth Century Calcutta,' Daruwalla depicts the large-scale death in Calcutta in the Nineteenth century, when people died of common diseases.

In a poem titled "The Parsi Hell" Daruwalla unambiguously states his death consciousness which is largely shared by Indians although the ages in the following words:

Throughout life a man carried his death
even as a woman carries her child.

If creation of a new idiom in English is one of the characteristics of post-colonialism, then Daruwalla's claim to be a post-colonial poet cannot be overlooked. He wants to use new idiom and create new themes by writing about contemporary Indian reality, subverting the tradition so that Indian English poetry will assume an identity of its own. In a poem called "The King Speaks to the Scribe," Daruwalla suggests:

Write whatever
you chance on. Don't look for a white-quartz boulder
Anything will do, a mass of trap rock
or just a stone sheet. And the language simple
something the forest folk can understand.

Good poetry is written in a live language, and this is not the age of great poets. Daruwalla reiterates this point in the following lines:

"...no hope for fresh words
from a tired language...

This is not the right age
for tall poets.

(*'Don't Expect'* A Summer of Tigers
1995: 50-51)

In the words of M.K. Naik and Shyamala A. Narayan, "the most impressive group of poems in *Night River* is the section, 'Stalking Mandelstam' which deals with the tragedy of the Russian poet, jailed for writing a satirical poem on Stalin in 1933. It is significant that perhaps the most appealing of these poems is 'Poem 8,' in which Osip Mandelstan himself speaks. This would once again indicate where Daruwalla's strength lies" (2001: 158).

R. Parthasarathy, who more than anybody else was instrumental in popularising Indian English poetry in mid-seventies, has not published any book of poetry after his *Rough Passage* in 1976. However, he has published some scattered poems in different journals and poetry magazines in the post-1980 era. He mostly writes in his favourite triplet-stanzas. He dives deep into the myths of our country and tries to reexamine them in the present context. In a poem titled "Ganesh" he tries to put Ganesh-myth in its perspective. If Lord Shiva after beheading Ganesha put the head of the elephant in its place, then there is a cause to worry about the elephant's life. Thus, he writes:

Ganesha's rashness cost him his head.

....

The Lord of Animals then planted
hastily an elephant's head on his son,
who rode off snoring
into the sunset on, of all things, a mouse

....

And no one ever bothered to find out
what happened to the elephant.
Whose head, you wonder, will role next?

(*Journal of Literature and Aesthetics*
1:1,2001:112)

G.S. Sharat Chandra was an expatriate Indian English poet like Ramanujan. And again like Ramanujan, he too died early. His three collections—*Heirloom* (1982), *Immigrants of Loss*

(1993) and *Family Mirrors* (1993) are significant contributions to Indian English poetry. The undertone of irony is pervasive in *Heirloom.* A sense of belongingness (or the lack of it) overwhelms them. To which country does an expatriate poet belong—the country of birth or adaptation? This situation is dealt with in a deft manner in G.S. Sharat Chandra's "In the Third Country." When a person dies, his dead body is given to his relations for last rites. In this poem a situation is contemplated in which man breathes his last and how his funeral is performed in a casual manner in different countries. In the country of his birth the last rites are performed according to his religion.

Thus the poet says:

In the Country that exiled you
it's a simple funeral
a mummy in white
you are carted off
to the ghats of Benares
in a wheel card.
In the presence of Sadhus
for a fee or for none. (15)

In the Country of his adaptation the funeral takes place in a very indifferent way. As the poet puts it:

In the country you went for
your ex-wife arrives
by the next available flight
the children as usual
are at the summer camp
For want of religious clarity
you are hearsed to the public cemetery
....
....
Your friends in Iowa bewail you in a bar
Someone reads a poem or two
Someone mentions you on the telephone. (26)

If this is the kind of treatment one gets in his country of birth and in the country of his domicile after his death, then one is completely ignored in a third country, where 'No one wants your whereabouts/no one worries your mail.' Though irony is implicit in this poem, it is not without pathos. Behind the appearance there lies the agony of recognition and longing for belonging, which explain the lack of ease with life.

In the words of Naik and Narayan, "Sharat Chandra is still preoccupied with the memory motif, but is, at the same time, moving in the new direction: a more objective kind of verse, with a marked dramatic element" (2000: 163).

O.P. Bhatnagar (1932-2001) who began his poetic career with the publication of *Thought Poems* in 1976, published four books of verse, *Angles of Retreat, Oneric Visions, Shadows in Floodlights and The Audible Landscape* in the post-1980 era.

Irony and humour are Bhatnagar's forte. He wrote topical poems and as a postcolonial poet laid emphasis on 'nation' and 'nativism.' His most well-known poem on the theme of brain drain is "Look Homeward Angel" which underlines the concept of 'nativism.' In this poem, Bhatnagar observes with the curiosity of an artist and the irony of a keenly critical mind, the implication of the exodus of the intellectuals of his country to foreign lands and makes a fervent plea to them to return home. The poet maintains an objective view and does not mind his friends—working in various fields in different countries like England, Mozambique, America and Australia; but it pains him when they perform 'cultural striptease' or are 'waltzing national pride.' He also comes heavily on those who glorify 'our sons/ settled abroad with merry relaxation.' Intellectuals living abroad betray their country, which 'once brought them up/splitting water with sunrays.' Bhatnagar compares them with migrating birds, and asks to dismiss the intellectuals as selfish who fail 'to look beyond glamour and gold.' The migrating birds that are 'forced out of home/at the turn of every season/return to their land/traversing incredible distance.' But our 'Heroes' (as he ironically calls them) are unlike Ulysses who 'brought his ships back home' and hence they 'make no myths.' The conversational tone and free verse and flowing lines make the reading of the poem interesting and enjoyable.

A.K. Mehrotra, Gieve Patel, Eunice de Souza, and Arun Kolkatkar published their new collection of poems in the 1980-era and enriched Indian English poetry. A.K. Mehrotra, who found a place in R. Parthasarathy's (ed.) *Ten Twentieth Century Poets* (1976), has grown remarkably in 1980s. He has published three volumes of poems, *Statute Miles* (1982), *Middle Earth* (1984) and *The Transfiguring Places* (1998) in the post-1980 era. Mehrotra is an imagist poet. M.K. Naik and Shyamala A. Narayan make an important observation on his later poetry in the following words:

> "Several poems offer reflections on life and art, reality and fantasy. An old family photograph on the wall of Mother's bedroom sets the speaker thinking; all those in the photograph are now dead, but the spiders that live in it/Are of a golden colour" ("The Photograph"), the relationship between art and reality is the subject of "The Vase That is Marriage," and not only is the daughter in 'To an Unborn Daughter' a creation of fantasy so is her mother: 'I saw her/only once, through a train window/In a yellow field."

Mehrotra's imagery is no longer bizarre, though it maintains its usual quality, as in "A heron shooting off his mouth" and "A wind raises in the octave branches." *Transfiguring Places* registers a distinct advance over Mehrotra's earlier verse (2001: 155).

In one of the poems included in *Middle Earth,* Mehrotra lays emphasis on understanding of his own mind, which seems to me an important trait of his poetry. He writes:

> There's a mountain in my mind,
> I must be true to it
> There's a mountain in
> My Mind and I
> Must read it
> Line by
> line. ("The World's a Painting House")

Gieve Patel who found a place in R. Parthasarathy's anthology, *Ten Twentieth Century Indian Poets,* has published new anthology of poems titled, *Mirrored Mirroring* (1991) in the last decade of the twentieth century. This is an improvement over his carlier collections, particularly, *How Do you withstand Body* (1976). M.K. Naik and Shyamala A. Narayan made an interesting observation on *Mirrored Mirroring:* "Poetry of reflection like this has naturally little use for the situational strategy, which, however, still dominates poems which operate of a mundane level. In "From Bombay Central," the spectacle of the long-distance train makes the speaker capture the varied sights and sounds his mind registers, without straining after allegorical flourishes. On the other hand, the sight of squirrels in Washington, which approach you boldly but halt some feet away, sets the poet thinking about a possible "hierarchy of distance" between creatures in the universe, the non-observance of which "would at once/Agglutinate all of Nature/Into a messy, inextricable mass."

Patel has always used imagery sparingly (a curious trait in a poet who is also a noted painter); but that makes the sudden appearance of a telling image all the more effective as in "heraldic shafts of sunlight" and "Give/With frost in the heart" (2001: 153).

Eunice de Souza (1940-) is a much-anthologised poet. Her first collection of poems, *Fire* (1979) is followed by three more collections, *Women in Dutch Painting* (1988), *Ways of Belonging* (1990) and *Selected and New Poems* (1994) in recent years. She began her poetic career as an ironist but soon outgrew that stage by looking at life with objectivity and compassion. She understands women well and looks at them from a woman's point of view. Thus, she says,

> The afternoon sun is on their faces
> They are calm, not stupid, pregnant, not bovine
> I know women like that
> and not just in paintings—
>
> ('Women in Dutch Painting')

Again in "Advice to Women," she calls upon women to tolerate 'the otherness of lovers' and have patience for their return. As she puts it:

> Keep Cats
> if you want to learn to cope with
> the otherness of lovers.
> Otherness is not always neglect —
> cats return to their litter trays
> when they need to. ('Advice to Women')

A new generation of poets who made their mark in the Indian English poetic scene in the post-1980 era include the names of Vikram Seth, Bibhu Padhi, Makarand Paranjapee,

R.K. Singh, Manohar Sethy, Shanta Acharya, Prabhanjan K. Mishra, Niranjan Mohanty, Ranjit Hoskote, E.V. Ramakrishnan, Hoshang Merchant, C.P. Surendran, Tabish Khair and a few others.

Vikram Seth's (1952-) reputation as a novelist far outweighs and overshadows his position as an Indian English poet in the post-1980 era. He has published three collections of poems titled *Mappings* (1981), *The Humble Administrator's Garden* (1985), which won the Commonwealth Poetry Prize for Asia and *All you who Sleep Tonight* (1990), on the basis of which we can accord him the place he deserves among post-1980 Indian English Poets. Makrand Paranjape considers him to be a representative Post-1980 Indian English poet. He writes:

> "In fact, I consider his silent and unnoticed first book, *Mappings* (1981) to be the turning point in recent IE poetry, signalling the end of Modernism, and the beginning of a new period. Mapping was published privately by Seth in 1980 when he was a graduate student in California. Publisher after publisher had turned it down, forcing Seth to resort to this extreme and humiliating form of self-broadcasting. The next year, during his visit to India, P. Lal of the Writers Work offered to published the book. This in 1981, was born, in rather humble and obscure circumstances, one of the most successful literary careers of modern India" (*Chandrabhaga* 2/2000:84).

'Panipat,' the very first poem in the collection deals with the question of identity and the theme of nativity. His determination is to be rooted in his soil, 'I must be home at last.' M.K. Naik and Shyamala A. Narayan make an interesting comment on *The Humble Administrator's Garden* in the following words:

> "*The Humble Administrator's Garden* (1985) comprises three sections, named after a tree, each from three countries: "Watang" represents China; "Neem," India and "Live-Oak," the U.S.A. The "China" poems are obviously based upon Seth's experience of that country, as a research student. They are mostly descriptive, like the "India" poems. One gets the feeling that the poet is more at home in the U.S.A. than in the two other countries. There is a sense of immediacy here as when

the poet describes the boiling over a soup on the stove
or suddenly realises "to make love with a stranger is
the best" (2001:172-73).

A memorable poem, "Soon" included in his book of poems titled *All You Who Sleep Tonight,* is both about love and death. It expresses the agony of a person who is going to die of a deadly disease and at the same time expresses his desire to be loved. The longing for life and the agony of death are finely poised together in this poem. This is how the poem begins and ends:

I shall die soon. I know.
This thing is in my blood.
It will not let me go.
It saps my cells for food.
. . .
Stay by my steel ward bed
And hold me where I lie.
Love me when I am dead
And do not let me die. ('Soon')

Bibhu Padhi (1951-) has published four collections of poems between 1988 and 1999. They are: *Going to the Temple* (1988), *A Wound Elsewhere* (1992), *Lines from a Legend* (1993) and *Painting the House* (1999). Padhi makes a 'voyage within' and describes situations and incidents of day-to-day life which are not only real but authentic. He makes us see into reality of joint-family life and secures the readers' participation. Important poems in this mode which deserve special mention are 'The House,' 'Letter to my Wife' and 'Grandmother.' In 'The House' Padhi tells us, how he is bound to it when his brothers have left for other places.

I've been here since the time
I learnt to know one house from another
There've been times when I thought
of leaving it altogether, forever.
Perhaps I'll never be able to do so.

This poem is reminiscent of A.K. Ramanujan's family poem, "Small Scale-Reflections on a Great House." In the same way Padhi writes:

Nothing moves here as though chained
to ancestral blemishes never forgiven.
No one visits us, not even my brothers.

They now live-in large cities,
in rented buddings, government quarters.
I don't blame my father, who put
all that he had saved into this house
in the hope his children wouldn't have to seek
Other houses.

This poem evokes a sentiment which is genuine, and authentic. The observation is very apt, and the tone is conversational befitting the theme. 'Grandmother' reminds us of Kamala Das' "My Grandmother's House." The memory of the grandmother is very poignant, and it is associated with events in life, one can never forget. Concern of a grandmother for the grandchildren and other members of the family and children's love for her evoke the atmosphere of a family in its realistic terms. Her warning:

"Take care of your child
You will never get another like him"

and the poet's son's affection for her has been described in an authentic manner.

...I watch my son
kiss her cold breathless hands
in his own small, childish way;

Padhi's title poems *Going to the Temple* (that is his first collection of poems) and *A Wound Elsewhere* are both evocative and suggestive in nature. While going to the temple, Padhi says,

Let us wash our hands clean
of the cruel day light
wipe the acquired and inherited
meanings off our tired faces.

The deep meaning of these lines is a dig at the way people worship mechanically or perform rituals. The transferred epithet 'cruel daylight' is ironical of our outward show of love and devotion to the deity. Padhi makes an attempt at new collocation of words like 'rooted grief ('Hamlet's Song'), 'Crowless Silence' ('Crow'), 'nightly dreams' ('Konarka') in his first books of verse. The title poem of *A Would Elsewhere* is reminiscent of Eliot's 'Burnt Norton' in its use of words and lines ('Not here, not here, not this, not here') and partly autobiographical (should we way, confessional?). The poetic persona seeks to find the wound that hurts him and brings to his mind the causes that might have created it—migraine, death of the father, nervous breakdown of 'still young mother,' erstwhile friends, son, brothers, losing faith—but to no avail. Then, he concludes:

> No one knows, no one need know.
> It is always some other lace—
> the hurt stealing into the might from there.

In his depiction of the agony of life, Padhi is with Shiv K. Kumar.

Bibhu Padhi's fourth book of poems, *Painting the House* (1999) marks the culmination of his themes and techniques employed in his first three books. He has combined something of Ezekiel and Ramanujan in this book of verse. For instance poems like "House Lizards" and "Portrait of a Family" remind us of Ezekiel's "Night of the Scorpion" and Ramanujan's "Small Scale Reflections on a Great House" in evoking natural scenes in Indian situation. House Lizards are said to be on the side of truth and therefore, believable. This is how Padhi puts it:

> They are believed to be right, always.
> When we differ on a critical point, from behind
> the piles of old newspapers will come the words:
> True, true.

They belong to reptilian group and are taken to be the 'preservers of ancient memories.'

"A Portrait of a Family" reflects on an aged old sick woman, whose husband and child are worried about her inevitable end. The man puts his hand on 'her cheeks, her forehead and lips/ over her fingers that look delicate still' to ascertain whether she is alive. The poem ends with the protagonist's longing for the old woman's long life:

> As I write this, I can almost hear a line
> travel back through the early sun and bird cries:
> You built this home and I only wish
> you had lived a little longer to see
> how, after you, it broke and crumbled—
> in spite of me, in spite of me.

Padhi's poetry is evocative in nature. The language is polished, neat, chiselled. In his use of language Padhi is with Ezekiel, Ramanujan and Parthasarathy. He is successful in acclimatizing an indigenous tradition to English language.

Like Ezekiel, Padhi tries to create poems out of ordinary things and insignificant insects or reptiles, which evoke in our mind the typical Indian scene in which we participate with empathy. For example, in a poem called "House Lizards" included in *Painting the House* mentioned earlier, Padhi depicts a scene in which we Indians listen to the 'true, true' sound of a house lizard and take it to be 'true.'

> In these tropical homes, they are many,
> but they keep mostly to themselves and eat only
> those insects who gratefully offer themselves...
> During a crisis in though, ...
> or when, at the lean lost end
> of an imaging hour, we find ourselves
> farther than we were, we hear:
> True, true.
> Reptilian group, cream-white and smoke-grey.
> Harmless. Preservers of ancient memories.
> Our wise forefathers in enviable disguise.

Padhi believes that creativity gives rise to the birth of new things. And therefore, he takes the critics to task who say theoretically that everything has already been said and we merely repeat what others have thought and imagined. In a poem titled, "Those Theories of Speech," he asks a pointed question and answers:

> They say all our speeches were there
> already, just as thoughts and meanings:
> there is nothing more or new to be said.
> Why then this urge to speak, why friends
> and new love, why the brief spring,
> the endless summer, the hunger, earthquakes?
> There must be something else too besides
> words and gestures, something not heard
> nor seen, nor read, not quite understood.

(Journal of Literature and Aesthetics,
July-Dec. 2001:143)

Shanta Acharya (1952-) who lives abroad has two collection of poems, *Not this, Not that* (1994) and *Numbering our Day's Illusions* (1995) to her credit. In her poetry there is a longing for serenity, and calm of mind. She tries to come to terms with herself. Eliot once said, 'People may change and smile but the agony abides.' This seems to be true in case of Shanta Acharya. Memory is a burden that needs to be overcome. Poem after poem she tries to redeem her past and come to terms with reality that baffles her. In "Highgate Cemetery" she says,

> In the unmapped terrain within us we busy
> in terraced catacombs painful memories.
> If only we could let them grow out of us like trees.

She harks on the same theme in another poem called 'Sleep.'

> It is terrible to live with memory
> the beginning of all our suffering.

With the advancing years comes the regret for the past and uncertainty for the future. Thus, she writes:

> I travel towards what end I cannot say—
> along the way, those I meet and those I don't,
> all that happens and all that I wait for to happen
> keep defining me in some inexplicable way
> Daily mirror mocks my wrinkles and streaks of grey.
> ('Shringara,' JLA Jan-June 1998:63)

The voice in her poetry is controlled and submerged, looking before and after.

Hence, the prayer to understand the meaning of life and bear sufferings with courage and determination.

> ...I have to pray and wait
> for life's meaning to unfold itself to me
> ('The Poet's RSVP')
>
> Teach me how to find myself in these palaces of art,
> that I may learn to love and suffer with my heart
> ('An Italian Prayer')

Apart from the thematic contents, the language is highly evocative of the scenes depicted in her poetry. The form in her poetry is controlled, and the choice of words and images is appropriate. Acharaya has contributed to the creation of an Indian English idiom by using innovative language in her poetry and that is not a mean achievement.

Meena Alexander is one of the well-known Indian English poets of post-1980 period, who has become an expatriate poet in recent years. Her poetry can be studied profitably along with the poetry of Sujatha Bhatt, Rukmani Bhaya Nair and

Ranjit Hoskott. She has four collections of poems titled *Stone Roots* (1980), *House of a Thousand Doors* (1985), *River and Bridge* (1995) and *The Shock of Arrival* (1996) to her credit. M.K. Naik and Shyamala A Narayan make an interesting observation on her poetry in the following lines:

> Alexander has been living abroad for a number of years, but her roots are firmly planted in her native Kerala soil. Hence, while reacting to her Western experience, her mind keeps on making an effortless transition to the Eastern Milieu. Thus, the speaker in "City Street" in the U.S.A. turns for a simile to "a burnt dosa on a griddle/idlis wasting in steam"; and at the "edge of San Andreas Fault," her persona remembers the "tin pins you get/a paise a dozen in Moor Market." From Central Park, New York, to Deer Park, Sarnath, is but a short step for her.

A strong political awareness is another striking feature of Alexander's poetry, and this is a trait which few of the contemporary women poets share. In "News of the World," a woman from Cambodia remembers how during the political trouble there, "I/my mother's head in a sack/ ran three days and nights/through a rice-field." "The Young of Tiananmen" is a moving tribute to martyrs of the notorious Tiananmen Square massacre, "as blood swallowed them whole." "Prison Cell" is an imaginative reconstruction of Nelson Mandela's experience in prison, where "even an ant, a fly/would be company." The poet also writes about Safdar Hashmi,

> The Marxist playwright, who was killed by a mob while performing a street play in support of striking workers. Her keen political conscience makes note of "Turks burnt alive in Germany;" a Muslim woman in Sarajevo shot to death; a man in Somalia "locked to his starving child," and "Hundreds hacked to death in Ayodhya/in Ram's (sic) golden name" (2000:194).

In a poem titled "Diary of Dreams," Alexander recollects the charge that has taken place in India during the period between Gandhian Movement for freedom and now. She writes:

> Before my birth
> a republic was burnt

fought with prayers burnt
indigo, and steel.

Gandhian ideal of nonviolence has yielded place to nuclear explosion for defence preparedness now. Thus, she regrets:

In Pokhran's desert
a bright bomb
carves soil
into feverish ruins
The wind is slow
torn leaves variable.
Truth has a deeper hold
than perishing. (*Chandrabhaga* 1/2000:28)

Sunita Jain (1940-) is a bilingual writer who writes both fiction and poetry in Hindi as well as in English. Apart from her three volumes of poems written before 1980, she has published five collections of poetry such as *Lovetime* (1980), *Silences* (1982), *Find Me with Rain* (1984), *Till I Find Myself* (1986) and *Sensum: Collected Poems: 1865-2000* (2000). She is primarily a love poet who looks at it from both the angles—positive and negative. She is also known for her innovative imagery such as 'hair' being likened not to 'golden wires' (Elizabethan imagery) but to 'school children in a file.'

Sujata Bhatt (1956-), a promising poet has a number of collections of poems to her credit such as *Brunizem* (1988), *Monkey Shadows* (1991), *The Striking Rose* (1995), *Point No Point: Selected Poems* (1997) and *My Mother's Way of Wearing a Sari* (2000). A widely travelled poet, she reflects on her experiences both inside the country and abroad in her poetry. M.K. Naik and Shyamala A. Narayan make an interesting point on her poetry in the following lines:

> She is as much interested in Sujata (her namesake), the first woman disciple of the Buddha, as in Eurydice; the massacre of the Sikhs in Delhi in 1984 moves her, and so does the Soviet invasion of Afghanistan. And we find her spending a whole day with buffaloes and goats in a Gujarat village and later ten "how-do-you-do minutes" in Iowa City, U.S.A.

This is probably why Bhatt seems to be obsessed with the question of language, which she looks at from different points of view at different times. Aware of the limitations of language, she confesses:

> The best story, of course,
> is the one you can't write
> you won't write
> it's something that you can only live
> in your heart,
> not on paper. (2001:196-97)

Her three poems, "Self-portrait with Coppery Red Hair," "Self-portrait as Aubade" and "Self-portrait with a Hat and Veil" reveal her talent for imagery and aptness of observation. For example, she employs striking images like "The fire is in your hair" and "moonstone skin" in her poetry. She also uses archetypes to portray the mind of the protagonist in "Self-portrait with a Hat and Veil."

> In this hat and
> veil in this sheet yellow veil
> I am Eurydice?
> in hell—
> ....
> Pinkish lavender: the last two roses
> orpheus left behind
> for me—If only he had
> given me flowers that were white
> or even yellow—
> Then I wouldn't
> feel so conspicuous
> *so out of place.* (*Journal of Literature and Aesthetics* 1:1, July-Dec. 2001:124)

Rukmini Bhaya Nair (1952-) has two collections of poems, *The Hyoid Bone* (1992) and *The Ayodha Cantos: Poems* (1999) to her credit. Her command of language and fascination for linguistic skill are evident in the first book of verse. The second book is written against the backdrop of Babri Masjid demolition in December 1992. In this volume, "the poet has evidently bitten off more than she has been able to chew properly. Neither the 'prelude' nor the 'post-script' is organically connected with the cantos and the poem seems to suffer from a basic confusion," say Naik and Narayan (2000:199). Four of her new poems

('Seasons,' 'Kali,' 'The Third Eye' and 'Buddha') were published in *Journal of Literature and Aesthetics* (July-Dec., 2001, 116-17), which reveal her talent as a poet. In "seasons" she integrates woman's mind with nature that controls the seasons.

Thus, she writes:

> Some write to remember, others
> To forget
>   But when the vagrant
> winds of autumn sweep
> Into a woman's mind
> she writes
>   To surrender, she wants
>   To be met. ('Seasons')

Makarand Paranjape (1960-) is a promising poet. He is essentially a poet of love and his two volumes of poems, *The Serene Flame* and *Playing the Dark God* contain a good deal of love poems. M.K. Naik and Shyamala A. Narayan have given a cue to the understanding of his poetry in the following lines:

> The Serene Flame follows the course of love from wide-eyed adolescence to conjugal maturity, until the eternal wrestling with "this angel/devil called love makes the lover realize that Love, like Nirvana, is something to "strive towards/But never attained."

The quest continues in *Playing the Dark God,* but if the poet takes us through the same woods, it is into wilder and darker regions, as he ponders post-marital perplexities. In doing so, he substitutes the predominantly lyrical mode of *The Serene Flame* with a more objective strategy, presenting his theme as a dramatic sequence in three acts. The protagonist sees himself as a latter-day Krishna (The Dark God), forever busy with "affairs and indiscretions," "grand passions and betrayals," and he views women in different roles: woman as shy virgin, coy mistress, former flame turned happy housewife in another's home, seductive siren—in fact, women playing different parts as Kanyakumari, Radha, and Gopi opposite the eternally young Krishna (2000:178-79).

Paranjape's two interesting poems "The Homecoming" and "Torsos" cleanly show the merit of poet and his competence of image building. In "The Homecoming," the protagonist comes back to India, only to die a peaceful death. He plays on words and has a sense of humour and irony to make his poetry readable. A lady, who was doctor pronounced the protagonist dead because of cardiac arrest. This is how the poems proceeds:

> "He's had an arrest," she said. What? Has he been
> arrested?
> Someone blurred.
> No, no, it's cardiac arrest. It's all over.
>
> ('The Homecoming')

The ending of the poem is appropriate for it takes death as an affirmation of life. Thus, writes the poet:

> O' Lord!
> But it was the face that caught my attention.
> It looked so calm,
> serene and relaxed, with a soft smile on the lips.
> It was the picture
> of a happy man whose last wish had been to come back
> home todie.
>
> (*Journal of Literature and Aesthetics*,
> *1:1 July-Dec. 2001:135*)

Paranjape's critical insight merges with his creative faculty to produce a well thought out poem like 'Used Book.' It is a commonplace observation that some readers make pencil marks on the margin of the book while reading it. But Paranjape tells us how these marks guide the successive readers to take the text in its proper perspective. He too wants to add some more comments to it without erasing the former reader's pencil marks so that his successor will be benefited from it. In other words, the pencil marks on the side of a text serve as a kind of criticism. Thus, he writes:

> Your pencil-strokes forbid relief;
> Withdrawing often, they reappear astutely
> To startle thought and remind.
> Who are you that note so decorously?
> That have left *your* slight initials
> On every peak of understanding?
> ....
> I shall not erase your caress
> Nor shall I uneasily dispossess your overtures,
> But adding my touch to yours

Mingling dark lead to dimming carbon,
I shall forge another generation of signs
And turn our book loose, once more
For its next textual tryst. *(An Anthology of New* Indian English Poetry *1993:76)*

Apart from the joint critical contribution hinted at by their pencil marks on the side of the book, there is also an overtone of sexual union between these two readers of the poem. The suggestive meaning or the deep meaning is more interesting in the context of the poem.

C.P. Surendran (1959-) is a promising poet. His first collection of poems, *Posthumous Poems* was published in Viking by Penguin Books India in 1999. It grew out of the failure of Naxalite Movement and Communism which deeply touched the heart of the poet. Coupled with it is the divorce of his first wife, which made him look for an escape route. Poetry provided that route and became a way of belief with him. Words have a special appeal for him. In a poem titled, "A Shortage of Words" he says:

I think now
Each blow to the body is a word
Deleted from the dictionary. That's why
We don't have more words than we deserve.

Like the poetry of Shiv K. Kumar, C.P. Surendran's poetry begins with pain and suffering, and one hopes, in course of time he will come to terms with life.

E.V. Ramakrishnan (1949-) has two collections of poems, *Being Elsewhere in Myself* (1980) and *A Python in a Snake Park* (1994) to his credit. Like most of the Indian English poets, he also writes topical poems. In 'Tremors' he writes about the Gujarat earthquake and describes how anxious he was to send the message of his safety to his mother. He writes:

'Mother, there was a tremour
here half an hour back...we are all
safe.' At that moment we didn't know
the quake had killed thousands and
many more lay trapped on the rubble.
(Journal of Literature and Aesthetics, 2001:138)

Niranjan Mohanty (1953-) and R.K. Singh (1950-) have published widely in the post-1980 period. Mohanty has published four collections of poems titled *Oh! This Bloody Game* (1980), *Prayers to Lord Jagannath* (1994), *On Teaching You and Other Poems* (1999) and *Life Lines* (1999) during the last two decades or so. He writes poems about contemporary life and there is an amalgam of disparate experiences embodied into the texture of poetry. His long poem "Prayer to Lord Jagannath" is a memorable poem.

R.K. Singh's *Above the Earth's Green* (1997) and *Cover to Cover* (2002) which contains the poems of R.K. Singh and U.S. Bahri are good collections of poetry which contribute substantially to the Post-1980 Indian English poetic movement. Like most of his contemporaries, R.K. Singh writes topical poems. Hence, the current state of affairs hurt him, like John Silkin who says, 'to think it hurts.' Singh says:

> It hurts to see my country die
> slowly and steadily after
> 50 years of self-rule
> ....
> the new rulers are blind
> to common man asking
> a fair share and honest rule. ('The Face in all Seasons')

Apart from the poets mentioned above there are some promising Indian English poets who have published their collections in the Post-1980 era. They are Prabhanjan K. Mishra, Niranjana Mishra, Ranjit Hoskote, Manohar Shetty, Sarbeswar Samal, Rabi Swain, Hoshang Merchant, P.K. Joy, Tabish Khair, Kavita Ezekiel (1953-), (Nissim Ezekiel's daughter), Imitaz Dharker, Melanie Silgrado, Leela Gandhi and a few others. Looking at the number of poets writing in the post-1980 era, one gets impressed by their output. But number is not all. The quality of poetry should be good. Speaking of the quality, Jayanta Mahapatra, a leading Indian English poet expresses his dissatisfaction in the following words:

> If you can get down to its essence, even a lowly potato would be poetic.... In India, in the Post-Independence era, innumerable collections of poetry written in English have appeared from various publishing houses.... It is an off situation, because more bad poetry is being published now than ever before in India history.

> And whereas our fiction has made a decisive impact on literary writing around the world, nothing very significant has been seen in the output of Indian poetry written in English" *(JIWE* 2000:3).

No doubt, Jayanta Mahapatra is right to a great extent, but the fact remains that at least ten to fifteen new poets (apart from the great masters of the nineteen seventies) in the eighteens have made their presence felt both at home and abroad. It is these promising new post-1980 poets along with the old poets, who continued to write during this period, have produced a substantial body of poetry worthy of reading.

I would like to make a small point in the penultimate paragraph on the nature of Post-1980 Indian English poetry. That is, during this period, we do not get other many long poems in English. On the other hand, we get many short poems on contemporary subjects. It seems that our poets lack inwardness with language, though they have academic competence in it. But nonetheless, our poets in English (*i.e.,* Indian English poets) are trying hard to use English creatively in our situation and have succeeded to a great extent in creating an Indian English idiom.

An overview of Postmodern Indian English poetry reveals that it has established a national identity in the global context. Use of myths and references to gods and goddesses, to Indian mythology and epics, and reflection on contemporary society give the necessary impetus to it to be identified as a viable literature in the present context. It successfully faces the challenges posed by Bhasa literatures at home and postcolonial literature abroad. It has successfully assimilated the Indian sensibility into its texture by employing various themes of contemporary interest and moreover, it has chosen the native Indian English as the medium of expression. On this basis Indian English poetry is different from African poetry, Australian poetry, Canadian poetry, Caribbean poetry and so on. The authenticity of Indian English poetry is beyond question. The 'locale' of this poetry is the whole of India, for it is read, and enjoyed by the English educated Indians all over the country. And it has become a subject of academic interest and found its way into the university curriculum.

Works Cited

Daruwalla, Keki N. (ed.). *Two Decades of Indian Poetry.* Ghaziabad: Vikas Publishing House, 1980.

Das, Kamala. *Only the Soul Knows How to Sing*. Kottayam: D.C. Books, 1996.

Mahapatra Jayanta. "The Decline of Indian English Poetry. " *Journal of Indian Writing in English* 28:1 (January, 2000).

Naik, M.K. and Shyamala A. Narayan (ed.). *Indian English Literature 1980-2000: A Critical Survey.* Delhi: Pencraft International, 2001.

Paranjape, Makarand. "The State of Poetry: Reflections on the Changing Identity of Indian English Verse." *Chandrabhaga* (2/2000).

——Ed. *An Anthology of New Indian English Poetry*. Calcutta: Rupa and Co., 1993.

Satchidananda, K. "Transcending the Body." *Only the Soul Knows How to Sing*. Kottayam: D.C. Books, 1996.

3

Postmodern Indian English Fiction

Of all the genres of Indian English literature, fiction is the most developed and well received one in the postmodern period both at home and abroad. With Arundhati Roy's Booker Prize Award Winning novel, *The God of Small Things* (1997) Indian English novel has won international recognition. I should hasten to add that earlier in the nineteen sixties and seventies novelists like R.K. Narayan, Raja Rao, Mulk Raj Anand, Arun Joshi, Anita Desai and a few others have won recognition both at home and abroad. But Indian English novel has not attracted the attention of readers in our country and abroad, the way it has done in the postmodern period. If Indian English poetry flourished in the mid-seventies, thanks to R. Parthasarathy, (the then editor of Oxford University Press) who popularized it by publishing a number of Indian English poets and his most significant anthology titled, *Ten Twentieth Century Indian Poets,* Indian English novel had its luxuriant growth in the hands of Amitav Ghosh, Upamanyu Chatterjee, Shashi Tharoor, Vikram Seth, Shashi Deshpande, and a few others in the nineteen eighties and after. Salman Rushdie's *Midnight's Children,* a novel that won Booker's Booker Prize can be said to be the epoch-making book that has revolutionalised Indian English fiction in the postmodern period. And yet I do not consider Rusdie as an Indian English Writer—he is a writer of Indian origin or diaspora and can be best described as British/American Indian writer.

G.N. Devy holds a similar view on the question of the identity of an Indian English writer:

> "I think, since Indian English fiction has now a sufficient number of texts to suffice the needs of its institutionalized teaching, it is desirable to leave out writers who have no stakes in the Indian society. In the past, V.S. Naipaul used to be included in this body for convenience—till he made many enemies in India by his crazy travelogues. Just as it is desirable to leave Naipaul out of our account, it is also desirable to leave out writers like Rushdie, Rohinton Mistry, and Bharati Mukherjee out of any consideration of Indian English literature. If the mere accident of birth were enough of a criterion, we could have happily included Kipling, Lawrence Durrell, and such others, and American literature would have included Pound and Eliot" (Bharucha and Sarang 1994:12).

Before taking up individual Indian English novelists for a discussion, let us examine the characteristics of Postmodern Indian English fiction. The first thing that strikes us is the broadening of the thematic range of Indian English novel. There is a shift in emphasis—we have moved away from the Gandhian era of village centrism to the city centrism of the post-Emergency era. The 'locale' has shifted from the village to the metropolis of our country and then abroad. East-West encounter which is explained in terms of hybridity in relationship by post-colonial critics, takes 'a space' in Postmodern Indian English fiction. When the world has become 'a global village,' no culture, or society is pure or insular today. That is why Indian English fiction now takes characters, situations both from inside the country and abroad into its orbit and develops them. Critics like Edward Said, and Homi K. Bhabha have inspired the novelists to write more and more about cultural encounter between the East and the West. The result is Vikram Seth's *The Golden Gate* and *An Equal Music.*

In the Post-1980 era love, sex, and marriage or the failure of it are some of the leading themes in Indian English novel. The description of love and sex is very bold and rather unconventional. Arundhati Roy's *The God of Small Things* contains chapters which to speak the least are outrageous and Shiv K. Kumar's *A River With Three Banks* depicts love and sex without any inhibition. So is the case with Manju Kapur's *Difficult Daughters*. Marriage as a social institution has lost its sanctity and relevance in the post-1980 era. Vikram Seth's *A Suitable Boy* is about match-making.

Lack of faith in religion and declining moral standard and behaviour are some of the predominant themes in postmodern novel. Corruption in public as well as private lives of individuals too appeals to our novelists, and they write novels on this theme. Employing national myths and making allusions to national epics like the *Mahabharata*, the new novelists in the eighties and after, write good novels as Shashi Tharoor has done in the *Great Indian Novel*.

Apart from love, sex, and contemporary reality, Indian English women novelists have also written feminist novels. The rights of women must be preserved, the women novelist seem to say. Take for instance, Shashi Deshpande's *That Long Silence*, a novel that seeks to bring men and women on par in our society. Women novelists assert the rights of women to live their life in their own way.

Let me begin with Amitav Ghosh, a novelist, full of promise, potentiality and magnificent achievement. His important novels include *The Circle of Reason* (1986), *Shadow Lines* (1988), *In An Antique Land* (1992), *The Calcutta Chromosome* (1996) and *The Glass Palace* (2000). Ghosh has employed the technique of Magic Realism *(i.e.,* realism plus fantasy) and carried forward the Rushdie tradition. Using this technique, Ghosh has tried to present a vision of life that is based on contemporary reality, and it is in this sense that he comes closer to Shashi Tharoor. As M.K. Naik and Shyamala Narayan have rightly observed:

> This dichotomy is illustrated in two well-known novels of this period: *The Circle of Reason* (1986), the first novel by Amitav Ghosh (b. 1956), and Sashi Tharoor's (b. 1956), *The Great Indian Novel* (1989), also a first novel. Ghosh's protagonist is a Bengali orphan called 'Alu' (potato) because his head is shaped like one. His real name is "Nachiketa," which reminds us of the enterprising young boy in *Katha Upanishad*, who pursues the god of Death, importuning him to reveal to him the secret of existence. Alu is forced to run

> away from his village, because he is falsely accused of being a terrorist. His peregrinations take him to the Middle East, moving as he does from al-Ghazira, a small Persian Gulf town to Cairo, the Sahara and finally Algeria (2001:46).

Amitav Ghosh shot into fame with the publication of his first novel, *The Circle of Reason* in 1986. Apart from his Bengali background, his knowledge of Bangladesh, London, and Middle-East helped him to give a realistic touch to his novels. The places in his novels are not imaginary lands but places that can be located on the maps of the world. The novel has three stories woven around three characters. First section, 'satwa' ('Reason') revolves around Balaram, the second section, 'Rajas' ('passion') revolves around Zindi and the third section, 'Tamas' ('Death') centres around Mrs Verma. It is due to Mrs Verma that Kulfi gets a proper funeral, defying rational scepticism. Finally, Alu, Zindi and Jyoti Das, the police officer leave for their destination with hope.

His second novel, *The Shadow Lines* for which he got the Sahitya Akademi Award for the year 1989, is a good example of 'Magical Realism.' The theme of the novel is restricted to the people of a very small cross section of an upper middleclass Bengali family. The orthodox Bengali family is depicted at three stages—before partition, after partition, and in recent times. The first part of the novel "Going away" deals with the family's exit from Dhaka during the riot ridden days of the partition and the second part, 'Home coming' deals with the grandmother's futile attempt to rescue her only living uncle 'Jethamosai' from their ancestral home surrounded by Muslim refugees who would become violent at times. Ghosh's originality lies in his depiction of Communal strife in Calcutta and Bangladesh. He seems to say that there is a very marginal difference between fiction and reality. The suggestion is that there is a 'shadow line' between reality and imagination. And 'reality' is multifaceted.

If the major themes of Ghosh's first two novels *The Circle of Reason* and *The Shadow Lines* is nationalism, political freedom and international relations, the themes of his third novel, *In An Antique Land* relate to religion, its meaning and practice, various religious traditions and inter-continental cultural intermingling. The scholar protagonist gathers a lot of information about various cultural ethics and practices. He brings out parallels among Hindu, Muslim and Jewish cultures. It is a story about Egypt told by a man who came from India, another antique land. S. Sengupta has given a brilliant exposition of the novel in the following paragraphs:

> "The book has two sets of characters, the one belonging to history whom Ghosh pursues indefatigably as a student of social anthropology, and the other belonging to the present whom the narrator encounters and around whom he builds his fictional world. Ghosh's achievement, like that of any gifted historical novelist, lies in his ability to extract from actual events a set of characters whose fictional identity is camouflaged by the plausible interaction with their environment and by their ability to appeal to the reader. Unifying the two sets is the thread of historicity— a post-colonialist's interpretation of the events encompassing eight centuries starting with the twelfth and ending with the operational Desert Storm.
>
> The main characters in the pre-colonial world are Abraham Ben Yiju, a Tunisian Jewish Merchant who came to India via Egypt and Aden, and his slave bomma who is from Tulunad of ancient India. Through these characters Ghosh portrays a world where man lived in harmony with man, where the gulf existing between people of different races and different cultures became meaningless as they met over the draw bridge of humanity. The pages devoted to that world spill over with light and colour—ordinary people bustle around laughing, talking and doing the most ordinary things. The main characters easily relate to this environment. It is a world of happy people, a world with no racial conflict, no feeling of alienation or hopelessness....
>
> If in the main plot of Abraham Ben Yiju and his slave the journey is towards the humane aspects of civilization, the journey in the sub-plot seems to be in the opposite direction towards guns and bombs and tanks of Western Imperialism Powers which spell ruin

> for all the world, especially for so many Egyptians stranded in Iraq during the Operation Desert Storm. It was these colonisers who erected the man-made barriers and introduced the deep schism between Hindus and Muslims based on such inessential customs as the burning of the dead, the absence of circumcision in boys and clitoridectomy in girls. This was the modern age they ushered in where brother betrays brother for thirty pieces of silver, cherished codes of ethics are compromised and commitments to larger causes are drowned under waves of cupidity. Ghosh writes about cunning and egotism and betrayal. But on a profounder level he also writes about the eternal yearning in man to go back to an idyllic world—a world that existed, for example, eight centuries ago" (Pathak 1997: 5-7).

In *The Calcutta Chromosome* (1996) Amita Ghosh pleads for the emancipation of women. He makes Mangala, a sweeper-woman the protagonist of the novel. He highlights women's problems and carves out a rightful place for them in the society. I concur with M. Adhikari when she makes a pertinent point on the novel in the following words:

> In a revolutionary move, all the female characters of the novel remains unattached. Marriage is no longer an institution of paramount importance for woman. They lead 'single' but successful lives, and no aspersions are cast on their 'singleness.' These women are not enamoured of the ideology of 'blissful marriage.' There is no reference to Mangala's family; the Countess and Mrs. Aratounian die enjoying their spinsterhood; Urmila has a family consisting of father, mother and brothers but she always remains an outsider, the death of Sonali's boyfriend, Romen Haidar, kills her dreams of domesticity for good; Tara and Maria, in New York, lead isolated lives; and Urmila's sexual desires roused by Murugan are drastically crushed by Murugan's admission that once he too had been a syphilis patient (183). It seems that in no way is patriarchal system able to undermine their confidence, that has been additionally encouraged by their economic self-sufficiency. They have been vested with power to lead individual and independent lives that can ensure a continuation of their

> mission. Women as "victims of economic scarcity" do not exist in the world of *The Calcutta Chromosome*. Although in actual life autonomy of thought and action is seldom granted to women and they remain trapped in the enclosure of patriarchy, the ideologies of marriage and economic dependence in the context of daily existence are deliberately disregarded in Ghosh's novel (Pathak 1997:197-98).

"Ghosh's latest novel, *The Glass Palace* is about the rise and fall of imperial powers in the twentieth century. It is located in different parts of Burma, Malaya and India and the characters of this novel belong to three generations. A lot of research has gone into the making of the book. The Author's Note clearly states the genesis of the novel:

> The seed of this book was brought to India long before my own lifetime by my father and my uncle, the late Jagat Chandra Datta of Rangoon and moulmein 'The Prince' as he was known to his relatives. But neither my father nor my uncle would have recognised the crop that I have harvested. By the time I started work on this book, the memories they had handed on to me had lost their outlines, surviving often only as patterns of words, moods, textures. In attempting to write about places and times that I knew only at second and third hand, I found myself forced to create a parallel, wholly fictional world. *The Glass Palace* is thus unqualifiedly a novel, and I can state without reservation that except for King Thebaw, Queen Supayalat and their daughters, none of its principal characters bear any resemblance to real people, living or deceased.
>
> Perhaps it was the very elusiveness of what I was trying to remember that engendered in me a near-obsessive urge to render the backgrounds of my characters' lives as closely as I could. In the five years it took me to write *The Glass Palace* I read hundreds of books, memoirs, travelogues, gazetteers, articles and notebooks, published and unpublished; I travelled thousands of miles, visiting and re-visiting, so far as possible, all the settings and locations that figure in this novel; I sought out scores of people in India, Malaysia, Myanmar and Thailand" (2000:549).

Through a gripping story of Rajkumar, an Indian boy and Dolly, an attendant girl of the royal couple in Burma, Amitav Ghosh narrates the story of the British rule in the South Asian countries. Upamanyu Chatterjee sought into prominence with the publication of his first novel, *English August: An Indian Story* (1992). Subsequently he published two more books, *The Last Burden* (1993) and *The Mammaries of the Welfare State* (2000). *English August: An Indian Story* has an appropriate title for it suits the hero's mentality and mood, particularly when the hero is alienated from his land and people. Both thematically and technically this novel breaks a new ground. The novel combines the consciousness of the novels of nineteen sixties and eighties—that is, the farmer's problems of uprooted self and the latter's hybridity and intellectual idiom. If the place of action of contemporary novels has shifted from the village to the urban area like towns and cities, this novel is an exception. The whole action of it takes place in three places—Delhi, Calcutta and Madras, a district township akin to R.K. Narayan's Malgudi. It depicts the encounter of an urban youth with provincial India and gives an account of a twenty-four-year-old I.A.S. trainee posted at Madna, which according to the protagonist is "Mad, No!" It realistically records the protagonist's sense of isolation, rootlessness and cultural dislocation. It also depicts identity crisis which is so common with the present-day youth. The lack of identity leads them to various defects in building up personality and psychological balance.

The protagonist belongs to the new generation called the "cola generation," "the generation that does not oil its hair," "generation of ages" and the generation that would love to "get AIDS because it is rampant in America." His uncle defines him as "you are an absurd combination," "a boarding school English literature education and an obscure name from Hindu myth." According to the author "he is one, with no special attitude for anything" (*English August* 3).

The protagonist, Agastya Sen, an I.A.S. officer aged twenty-four goes for a year's training in district administration to a small town called Madna only to be disillusioned with the system in the end. The power and authority of an I.A.S. officer *vis-a-vis* the politicians turn out to be illusory. Getting disgusted with the system, Ayastya Sen resigns from service and returns to Calcutta where his father, Madhusudan Sen lives as the Governor of West Bengal. At the surface level the novel can be taken as a satirical portraiture of Indian Administrative service but at the deep level it is about self-discovery. Chatterjee makes an attempt as it were, to bring everyday reality into the realms of fiction.

In this second novel, *The Last Burden* (1993) Upamanyu Chatterjee deals with the basic structure of Indian society— that is, the family. How the 'family' which was the nucleus of Indian Society all through the ages, has become "a burden" is the theme of this novel. It deals with an Indian middle-class family that settles down in a new place after the partition. Urmila and Shyamanand, both government servants are not very happy as a couple, as a result, their two sons, Burfi and Jamun grow up amidst endless parental bickerings notwithstanding their public school education. Burfi has a Christian wife named Joyce. And their two sons, Doom and Pista are irreverent to their grandparents. Urmila dies of heart attack and Shyamanand chooses to live with his other son, Jamun who considers it 'not a bad beginning' as is indicated in the closing line of the book.

The Mammaries of the Welfare State reveals the grim reality that encompasses a country, where the poor and the downtrodden lead a miserable life. People at the helm of affairs enjoy their life and are insensitive to miseries of the underprivileged class.

Shashi Tharoor is a major novelist in the post-1980 period with three novels such as *The Great Indian Novel* (1989), *Show Business* (1994) and *Riot* (2001) to his credit. *The Great Indian Novel,* modelled on the *Mahabharata* is an ironic portrayal of the contemporary Indian political situation. Tharoor makes use of a national myth to create a contemporary novel. Thematically, the novel focuses on the striking parallels between the great epic battle as depicted in *The Mahabharata* and historic freedom struggle and post-Independence political manoeuvring in our country. While trying to yoke the national myth to contemporary reality. Tharoor is conscious of being accused of erring against proportion—a charge often made against the eighteenth-century writes. Thus, comes the apologetic note about the title of the novel:

> A hasty note of disclaimer is due to those readers who may feel, justifiably, that the work that follows is neither great, nor authentically Indian, nor even much of a novel. *The Great Indian Novel* takes its title not from the author's estimate of its contents but in defence to its primary source of inspiration, the ancient epic, *The Mahabharata.* In Sanskrit maha means great and Bharata means India.

The Great Indian Novel is a satirical portrayal of the political history of modern India from colonial era to the nineteen eighties when Indira Gandhi came back to power with a thumping majority after the Emergency debacle. With the progress of the novel, one finds Ved Vyasa (V.V) telling Ganapati about a number of subjects relevant to modern India in a jocular and hillarious manner. It seems as if Indian history is re-written from a different perspective.

Show Business (1991) is a different kind of novel. It is about Bollywood. Ashok Banjara, the protagonist of the novel, the superstar of the Silver screen bears resemblances of Amitab Bachan. Ashok while shooting meets with a serious accident and being taken to the hospital fights for his life in the intensive care unit. Prayers are offered by several people at several places for his recovery. Allusions to Amitab Bachan's accident while shooting the *Coolie* and prayers offered for him all over the country are there for any discerning reader to see.

Shashi Tharoor's third novel, *Riot* centres round the mysterious murder of Priscilla Hart, a young American lady who came to India to participate in a woman's health programme. On the surface level she appears to be a victim of a communal riot between Hindus and Muslims. But at the deep level the mystery of murder becomes elusive. The reason and the consequence of the murder defy any simple answer. The theme of the novel goes beyond a usual communal riot and seeks to examine issues of complex nature such as religious fanaticism, cultural collision and above all, the trajectory of history.

Vikram Seth created history in more than one way. He is the first Indian English novelist to write a novel titled *The Golden Gate* (1986) in verse, for which he won the Sahitya

Akademi Award for the year 1988. Again he is the first Indian English novelist to get a fabulous amount of rupees two crores as advance for his epoch-making novel *A Suitable Boy* (1993) (I should hasten to add that money is not the criteria for judging the excellence of a work of art). *The Golden Gate* heralded a new era in Indian English fiction. John Hollander calls it "a brilliantly fashioned tale of life among a number of Bayaree "yuppies" and that it is never anything less than quaintly and most unqualifiedly marvellous" [*The New Republic* 195:2 (April 1986: 32)]. This novel reminds us of Byron's *Don Juan* or Puskin's *Eugene Onegin*. Susan Sontag compares *The Golden Gate* to *Eugene Onegin* in its "particular mix of wit, sagacity and rue," and praises *The Golden Gate* as a thrilling, subtle literary achievement" (*American Poetry Review* Nov./Dec. 1986: 37-46). H.H. Anniah Gowda was full of praise for Vikram Seth, when he says that, "Vikram Seth has earned a place in the realms of gold. On reading *The Golden Gate* one tends to endorse the author's exclamation, 'How marvellously quaint'" (*The Literary Half-Yearly* 29:1, 1998:34). The novel is written in mellifluous sonnets and is devoid of oriental characters. It contains 594 stanzas, with a stanza each for acknowledgments, dedication, table of contents and a note about the author. It deals with the longing for love, affection and sense of belonging on the part of John, the Silicon Valley executive. Most of the characters experience loneliness in life and hence they search for meaning and emotional fulfilment. The happy ending of the novel, therefore, seems to be contrived.

A Suitable Boy (1993) deals with a simple theme, the quest for a suitable boy for Lata, the younger daughter of Rupa Mehra, Lata is a nineteen-year attractive girl, who has passed just her graduation. She has three suitors—Kabir Durani, Amit Chatterjee, and Haresh Khanna from among who she has to choose her life partner. Seth meticulously writes about these three suitors and Lata's affairs with each one of them, so that they can be judged objectively, and the final choice can be made. I concur with Jon Mee's analysis of A *Suitable Boy* made in the following lines:

Seth's novel is set in the early 1950s, formative years of the Nehru period with the passing of the *zamindari* legislation and the first election of the post-independence era looming. For all its copious realism, it is difficult not to see this novel too as an allegory of nationhood, where it differs from Rushdie's other literary children is in the confident way that it subscribes to an idea of Indian history as a progress towards the goal of a secular, commercial society in the image of conventional western models of national development. The novel is based on a romance plot, the choice of a suitable boy for the heroine Lata Mehra; but although she shows signs of independence, the novel is ultimately one of conformity and what it represents as the inevitability of bourgeois life. The man Lata chooses is neither the son of the Calcutta's high society, nor the Muslim boy whose friendship scandalises Lata's mother, but Haresh Khanna of Prahapore, a man who is foreign-returned but from a British technical college rather than the kind of elite institution which Seth himself attended. Moreover, it is the shoe trade for which he is being trained, a business profession which brings with it the spectre of the loss of caste. Haresh would seem to represent Seth's idea of properly bourgeois man emerging from religious superstition and social snobbery. In this respect, Seth's novel is very much an enlightenment history (Chakrabarty, 1995). Typically of such histories of progress, along with its sense of the inevitability of a particular kind of national development—for Haresh's success is surely intended as a parable for the times—comes a nostalgia for a feudal world of Urdu literature and country entertainments. *A Suitable Boy* would seem to affirm the idea that the destiny of middle-class India lies in casting aside an obstructive concern with traditional identities in pursuit of secularism in its liberal economic mode. With such confidence about the future of the nation, what is to be left behind can be romanticised in a nostalgia for a world that it views as inevitably lost. (Nanavati and Kar 2000: 47-48)

Seth's third novel, *An Equal Music* was published in 1999. In the authorial note included in the novel, Seth states:

> Music to me is dearer even than speech. When I realised that I would be writing about it I was gripped by anxiety. Only slowly did I reconcile myself to the thought of it (1999). It may be mentioned here that music is also the theme of two other contemporary Indian English novels— that is, Rushdie's *Ground Beneath her Feet* (1999) and Shashi Deshpande's *Small Remedies* (2000).

The title, *An Equal Music* is taken from John Donne's Sermon describing life after death. In heaven there will be, "no sun nor darkness nor dazzling but one equal light, no noise nor silence, but one equal music." Regarding the epigraph John Carey writes:

> But an epigraph might have been taken from another great English poet, Tennyson: 'Deep as first love, and wild with all regret.' Seth's story of love and loss can hold its own the vicinity of that marvellous line (*The Sunday Times* 2 April 1999).

The story of the novel opens in London with an upcoming musician, Michael Holme, a 35-year-old violinist from Rochdate playing with the Maggiore Quartet and giving music lessons to a group of not-so-enthusiastic pupils with one of whom he is carrying on a desultory affair. The novel has a turbulent love story full of passion and pathos. Seth has successfully integrated this love story with the story of music and music lessons. The novelist seems to say that music can alleviate the sufferings in life caused by the unfulfilled love. Hence, ending of the novel kindles a hope in human heart:

> Music, such music, is a sufficient gift. Why ask for happiness; why hope not to grieve? It is enough, it is to be blessed enough, to live from day to day and to hear such music —not too much, or the soul could not sustain it—from time to time (1999:381).

Vikram Chandra who won Commonwealth prize for his book short stories, titled, *Love and Longing in Bombay,* has a brilliant novel, *Red Earth and Pouring Rain* (1995) to his credit. The novel is a combination of history and myth, with the digressions of the epic. As the blurb of the book puts it:

> In Vikram Chandra's astonishing first novel, the gods: Hanuman, Ganesh and Yama descend on a house in an Indian City to vie for the soul of a wounded monkey. A bargain is struck: the monkey must tell a story, and if he can keep his audience entertained, he shall live. The result is *Red Earth and Pouring Rain,* a tale of nineteenth century India: of Sanjay, a poet, and Sikander, a warrior of hoofbeats thundering through the streets of Calcutta and the birth of a luminous child; of great wars and love affairs and a city gone "mad with poetry." And woven into this tapestry of stories is a second, totally modern narrative, the adventures of young Indian Criss-Crossing America is a car with his friends, and his eventual return to his homeland.

It is a novel in which gods and human are depicted as characters along with a monkey who was a Brahmin boy in his previous life. The characters include Hindu gods—Hanuman, Ganesh and Yama—and historical personages like de Boigne, head of Scindia's artillery, George Thomas and Begum Samru, both reputed adventurers, and it is they who participate in the fantastic events in the novel. I am inclined to agree with Jon Mee's analysis of the novel given in the following paragraph:

> The story of *Red Earth and Pouring Rain* revolves around the fate of Sanjay, reincarnated as a monkey that Abhay shoots for stealing his new jeans from the washing line. When Yama, god of death, enters, the story to claim the dying monkey, Ganesh intervenes with a deal. If Sanjay can tell his story and keep everyone entertained, then he will be saved. His story begins in the period when mercenaries and princes, along with the East India Company, were fighting over the remains of the Mughal Empire. Chandra's fictional characters mix not only with gods, but also historical figures like Begum Samroo and James Skinner. History in the novel becomes 'The Big Indian Life,' but he warns, "do not think that this story is untrue, because it is *itihasa,* thus it was." In the novels of Rushdie, Sealy, Ghosh and Kesavan, this idea is made the centre of a political inquiry into the ownership of stories, an aspect of the new historical novel which seems

> absent from Chandra's sense of history as 'Leela, the great cosmic play.' What Chandra does do, like Sealy in *The Trotter-Nama,* is to explicitly differentiate his method from a western tradition identified in terms of an Aristotelian desire for straight-lines and defining essences. In response, Chandra offers the familiar trope of India-as-heterogeneity, but one of the novel's strengths is that it does not simply produce an exoticised spectacle of otherness for a western readership. Abhay, the foreign-returned student, has to step into the gap created when Sanjay is too exhausted to continue by telling a tale of his scholarship days in America 'the crucible in which the world's most weightless and alluring myths are perfected.' The crowd who gather to listen remain as fascinated by this tale drawn from an entirely different mythology, a road movie which takes them across desert skies and into the big city of Houston, as by Sanjay's story of fantastic deeds from India's past. Western modernity is in this way reproduced not as the privileged sphere of truth and reason, but as the site of another mythology which is just as enticing as India's own—a perspective Chandra's novel shares with Sealy's travelogue, *From Yukon to Yucatan* (Nanavati and Kar 2000:46-47).

The Magic Realism technique popularised by Salman Rushdie attracted a large number of novelists of the Postmodern era (we may call them new generation novelists) such as Rukun Advani, Mukul Kesavan and Makarand Paranjape. *Beethoven Among the Cows* (1994) by Rukun Advani, *Looking Through Glass* (1995) by Mukul Kesavan, *The Narrator* (1995) by Makarand Paranjape, *An Angel in Pyjamas* (1996) by Tabish Khair, *Bombay Duck* (1990) by Farukh Dhondy, *The Memory of Elephants* (1988), and *Asylum, U.S.A.* (2000), both by Boman Desai are some of the important novels written in the technique of Magic Realism. I would like to quote here M.K. Naik and Shyamala A. Narayan for their apt comments on *Beethoven Among the Cows* and *The Narrator:*

> "The Magic Realism technique may give the novelist the widest possible scope for the exercise of imagination, but in that process, he always stands in danger of

losing his hold on the structural values of fiction. This is what happens in *Beethoven Among the Cows* (1994) by Rukun Advani (b. 1955). The eight chapters of the book are actually so many separate short stories linked together loosely by the two protagonists who are twins, and all the events are seen through their consciousness. The action covers a period of three decades, from 1962, the inglorious year of the war with China, when the twins are born, to 1992, which witnessed the infamous demolition of the Babri Masjid. The fantasy produces strange results: Elizabeth Taylor comes down from the cinema screen to meet the twins, and later, she suddenly merges into the historical Eliza Taylor, who was in the besieged residency in Delhi during the Mutiny of 1857. The comedy operates at various levels, the most notable of which is the stylistic one. Advani makes deft use of parody, caricature, witty allusion and word-play. The character of Professor Lavatri All-theori, "the Moby Dick of the American Academy" is of topical interest, as a caricature of a well-known modern Indian critic long settled in the U.S.A. We are told that in her Women's Movement, "Lit.crit" becomes "Lit.Clit." In the absence of a hard, central core, however, *Beethoven Among the Cows* remains a charismatic chaos of a book" (2001:50).

About The Narrator they have this to say:

"Embarking on a fantasy is like riding a tiger, you can't dismount without being doomed; *The Narrator* (1995) by Makarand Paranjape (b. 1960) demonstrates this truth. The narrative opens promisingly, with the protagonist, a University Lecturer in English undergoing a most curious experience: there is a sudden emanation from his mouth, which soon assumes a transparent human shape. It is probably his own uninhibited self. He calls it 'Baddy' (suggesting both "buddy" and "Biddy"—a short form of "Libido"). It is soon transmogrified into Badri(nath), a self-made businessman who proposes that the narrator and he should author a film script together. After this, the story of the film, the doings of the narrator and the going on of Baddy get mixed up until one is left wondering which is the text and which are subtexts" (*Ibidem.* 51-52).

Kiran Nagarkar own Sahitya Akademi Award for his historical novel, *Cuckold* for the year 2000. Cuckold is a different kind of novel, the like of which we don't find in Indian English literature. It is a culmination of history and legend, artistically woven into the framework of fiction. Nagarkar has done a good deal of research in Rajput history to write the novel. The time of the novel is the sixteenth century India, and the locale is the Rajput Kingdom of Mewar. The novelist has made an attempt to resituate the text in the historical context. The protagonist is Bhojraj, Meerabai's husband and the novel is depicted from his point of view in the first-person narrative. The canvas of the novel in vast—it encompasses four kingdoms: Rajput Kingdom of Mewar (Capital: Chittor), Muslim Kingdom of Gujarat (Capital: Ahmedabad), Muslim Kingdom of Malwa (Capital: Mandu), Muslim Kingdom of Delhi (Capital: Delhi)— and the characters of the novel are drawn from history. It contains 49 chapters with an 'Epilogue,' 'Afterword' culminating in the closing 'Historical Note.'

> The beginning of the novel is dramatic, for it re-enacts the dhobi myth in the *Ramayan* and the protagonist is bewildered to hear the complaint of an old bent dhobi's against his wife.
>
> An old, bent dhobi, I would have sworn it was the same Washerman who besmirched Sita's name and obliged Lord Rama to banish her into the wilderness some two thousand years ago, was now casting aspersions on his wife's virtue.
>
> 'She has a lover, may be several: his voice was thick with chronic bronchitis, and he had to clear his throat many times before he could speak.'
>
> Do you? I asked his wife. She couldn't have been more than sixteen or seventeen. How naive or hypocritical, can one get in Court? Did I really expect her to smile demurely and tell the court who she was sleeping with? (1).

Maharaj Kumar, (Bhojraj) was the eldest son of Rana Sanga (Maharana), the King of Mewar and heir apparent but Queen Karmavati, the Rana's favourite queen favoured her son Vikramaditya for the crown. So there was opposition to the protagonist within the family to succeed to the throne. Apart from that, the Rajput Kingdom of Mewar was locked in war with the Sultanates of Delhi, Gujarat and Malwar.

Maharaj Kumar's love for the Princes remains intact, her love for the Deity notwithstanding. There are moments of illusion in his life but ultimately he decides to be united with her. Mangla Sinha's (the head of the Intelligence) letter and his mother's (Kausalya's) letter to Maharaj Kumar bear testimony to it. Mangala's letter unfolds the plot hatched to annihilate the heir apparent.

"Your Highness. I suspect the very worst is about to befall Mewar. There is a plot under foot to murder. His Majesty and you. Do please take the most extreme measures to safeguard both your lives" (597-98).

Kausulya's (Kausalya was Maharaj Kumar's 'Dai') letter is more revealing and significant to understand the plot of the novel and the character of the protagonist. She writes:

> You were Mewar's and my great hope. The future of Mewar belonged to you. You were mine but my ambitions for you were my ambitions for our country.... I had prepared myself for your marriage from the day I first breast-fed you. But nothing could have prepared me for the princess. She was a devoted wife but not to you. It took me a long time to realise this, but I finally understood that she would destroy Mewar. The saddest part in all this was the influence she had over you. You seemed to lose your mind when you were with her. She would not give you a son and she made you the laughing-stock of Mewar.... I warned the Princess and asked her to mend her ways. She paid me no heed. I decided to take action.... I planned the Princess' death far more meticulously. I also took great care not to be caught. I poisoned her food as well as mine except that the dose I gave was a least ten times, stronger than the one I had. Since I was also a victim, nobody suspected me. Unfortunately I too did not succeed in ridding Mewar of the Princess.... The legend of the Little Saint *(i.e.,* Meera Bai) will become greater with every passing year. The whole world loves a lover, love and overheated poetry will make her immortal. As for

> you, Highness, if Queen Karmavati and Vikramaditya didn't get you, the Princess and her lover will. Either way, they will wipe out your memory. Can you break with your wife? Only then will you be able to get the better of your brother and his mother and concentrate on Babur and our other enemies....
>
> "There is only one women for you. It is the princess. It would have helped if she had loved you too. But no matter. You seem to do it for both of you" (599-600).

The protagonist appreciates Kausalya's words, but he knows that he cannot leave his wife. Like Antony in Shakespeare's play, *Antony and Cleopatra* the Maharaj Kumar knows that 'Kingdoms are clay.' Hence, the resolution:

> But there is one woman for me. It is not Leelawati, (Finance Minister Adinathji's granddaughter) and it is not Kausalya. It is my wife. I will follow her to Brindaban, to Mathura, to the gates of hell, even to heaven if the gods will have me (600).

In the epilogue, Nagarkar writes that Maharaj Kumar ran to the temple of the Flautist at Baswa being pursued by six men, and finally disappeared. The closing of the novel awakes a curiosity in the minds of the readers.

> It was then that the Flautist embraced the Maharaj Kumar. Terror and astonishment struck the six men. One minute the Maharaj Kumar was there, the next he had become invisible. Had they been dreaming! There was just the end of the Maharaj Kumar's turban, the Kesariya bana, showing outside the lower left edge of the Flautist's Chest (602-03).

This is one of the finest novels written in English in our time. Based on history and myth, the novel acclimatises our tradition and heritage to English language. It gives a lie to the critics who denigrate Indian English novelists and writers for what they call, the lack of 'authenticity' in their works. It is a novel about India's past which combines the historicity of fiction with fictionality of history. It richly deserves the Sahitya Akademi Award and perhaps, much more.

Apart from the new generation of writers writing in the nineteenth eighties, we have old generation of writers who have also written during this period. For example, R.K. Narayan, Mulk Raj Anand, Arun Joshi, and Shiv K. Kumar have published excellent novels in the post-1980 era.

R.K. Narayan has published four novels during the post-1980 period: *The Tiger for Malgudi* (1983), *Talkative Man* (1983), *The World of Nagaraj* (1990), and *Grandmother's Tale* (1992). Of these novels, only one—that is *The Tiger for Malgudi*—is a major novel.

Mulk Raj Anand published three novels during the post-1980 era. They are, *The Bubble* (1984), *Little Plays of Mahatma Gandhi* (1991) and *Nine Moods of Bharata: Novel of a Pilgrimage* (1998). Of the three novels only *The Bubble* to some extend repeats the success of Anand's earlier works like *Seven Summers* and *Morning Face.*

Shiv K. Kumar made his mark as a novelist with the publication of his first novel, *The Bone's Prayer* in 1979. Subsequently, he published three more novels titled, *Nude Before God* (1983), *A River With three Banks* (1998) and *Infatuation* (2001). Kumar's art of writing fiction is influenced by Joesph Conrad. He chooses his characters from among the people whom he knows and only charges the proper names to avoid controversy. An element of autobiography is clearly discernible, and he makes a confession of it in course of an interview given to Saraswati Sabu:

> I must confess that often I have written my stories with the names of original characters. That keeps me going; the characters are alive. I don't do it all the time. But it is said even of Tolstoy that for secondary characters he used the original names in the final version. Suresh Gupta is a real person I knew. He was a lecturer in History in Chandigarh when I was a lecturer in English there. The locale is Chandigarh. Similarly a critic asked me how much of myself I have included in *Nude Before God.* I told him he could not catch me, for I had written the letter to explain everything (1990:237).

A River With Three Banks deals with violence—the communal holocaust that followed the partition of India in 1947. As in E.M. Forster's *A Passage to India,* so in Kumar's A *River With Three Banks,* characters from three religions—

Hinduism, Islam and Christianity—are portrayed with insight and precision.

Arun Joshi won Sahitya Akademi Award for his novel *The Last Labyrinth* for the year 1982. Two of his five novels were published in the post-1980 period—*The Last Labyrinth* in 1981 and *The City and the River* in 1990. He is different from other Indian English novelists in his approach to life. What really sets him apart from others is his existential vision and attitude to human existence on earth. Exploration of the possibility of human achievement and search for identity forced him to lead a life of exile. Life and death are not mere binary opposites for him. He takes death not as a closer of life but a sad reminder of the inadequacies of it. Since death renders all human efforts futile, we have no other alternative than to turn to God for solace. Joshi believes that there is always a time in one's life when one turns to the Divine and 'becomes an instrument of God.' The all-pervading presence of God, is the conviction of his life and it is this conviction that binds his novels together. It is in this context, G.S. Amur makes a valid observation:

> Joshi's vision of the modern world and man's place in it is Manichean and his heroes though rooted in the industrial civilisation have always been at odds with it. It is for this reason that the action of his novels takes the form of a search for an alternative. His novels take us to the heart of darkness—one of his most favourite metaphors is the labyrinth—but he is not a prophet of despair. All his novels hold out promise of regeneration and redemption (1991:154).

The symbolic representation of the river in *The City and the River* suggests that the river is the source of life as she is the source of humanity and God is the ultimate Truth and 'His is the Will.' Having realised the importance of God in one's life, Joshi says that "the question in one's life is not of success or failure, but of trying."

Having discussed the major works in Indian English fiction written by men, I should now turn to Indian English fiction written by women in the postmodern period. Important women novelists who published their works in the postmodern period are Anita Desai, Nayantara Sahgal, Shashi Deshpande, Arundhati

Roy, Manju Kapur, Gita Meheta, Shobha De and Kamala Markandaya. All these writers wrote different kinds of novels though some of them use common method of writing fiction—that is, by inducting eroticism into their novels. The women novelists deal with the themes of love, marriage, loneliness and search for identity.

Kamala Markandaya published only one novel titled, *Pleasure City* (1982) after 1980. The novel is about the impact of the multinational corporation on villages. M.K. Naik and Shymala A. Narayan have given an outline of the novel in the following words:

> The cultural confrontation here is not the usual East verses West, it is tradition and modernity. An efficient multinational corporation comes to a sleepy fishing village on the Coromandel coast to built a holiday resort, Shalimar, the pleasure city; and the villagers, struggling at subsistence level, cannot resist the regular income offered by jobs in it. Markandaya gives a vivid picture of a fisherman's family: the old father, his elder son who scorns education, and Rikki, his adopted son, the hero of the novel, who has been educated by missionaries. Toby Tully, the manager, is descended from the Copelands and Tullys administrators under the Raj (Copeland was the sympathetic British official in *The Golden Honeycomb*, 1977). The minor characters too, such as Ranji, the young army officer proud of independent India, are vividly sketched, though Kamala Markandaya's infelicitous choice of names persists (2001:76-77).

Anita Desai published a number of novels such as *Clear Light of Day* (1980), *The Village by the Sea: An Indian Family Story* (1982), *In Custody* (1984), *Baumgartner's Bombay* (1988), *Journey to Ithaca* (1995) and *Fasting, Feasting* (1999) in the last two decades of the twentieth century. *Clear Light of Day* is about two sisters, Bimla and Tara. The novel begins with Tara's visit to Old Delhi, their ancient family home and ends with the departure of her family *(i.e.,* her husband and children). William Walsh gives an exposition of the novel in the following words:

> On the face of it *Clear Light of Day* is a delicate domestic study of the younger members of an interesting but not outstanding middle-class family. They are observed with sympathy and insight and their development is related in a poetic idiom charged with feeling and richly strewn with revealing analogies which make ordinary family life both dramatic and significant. The novel displays a high degree of professional competence, and it combines this skill with something more important, a creative idea. The initiating and sustaining conception have to do with the human experience which is both physical and spiritual, of an inner and an outer life. It has its origin in our physical and biological life in which space and distance are felt as they increase and extend to be more and more dangerous. Upon such space and distance society and tradition have imposed rituals of control, of which the most intimate are one's house and its surroundings, like the shabby house and unkempt garden which establish the limits of safety for Bim, Raja, Tara and Baba. Raja and Tara escape—as they see it—or desert as the others see it—the inner family space for an alien external life, Raja absolutely to become a rich Muslim's son-in-law and then as a fake Urdu poet, and Tara to marry a diplomat and to live the strange deracinated diplomatic life. Baba, at the other extreme from Raja, suffers from some genetic defect which makes it impossible for him to leave the nest. He never achieves that degree of autonomy that would enable him to work out a tolerable or even a tentative relationship between inner and outer worlds. The only one of the children who manages a scratchy uneven balance between the two is Bim, the surrogate mother of the handicapped Baba, the effective College lecturer, the chief if strained and worn prop of the family (1990: 114-15).

In Custody portrays the character of Deven, a temporary lecturer in Hindi in a private college nearly forty miles from Delhi. His pathetic life both at home and in the college makes him a pitiable character. He is also not above blame for he ill treats his wife and children. This novel is a realistic portrayal of the life of Deven who is 'more sinned against than sinning.

Baumgartner's Bombay depicts the plights of Hugo Baumgartner who remained a wandering Jew all his life. He had no sense of belonging to anywhere or anyone, and finally died a tragic death. The quest for identity is the main theme of the novel. The protagonist's early life in pre-war Berlin and then, in India *(i.e.,* in Calcutta and Bombay), where he lived for fifty years, could not solve the problem of his identity. In India he was called a, "Firangee foreigner." Ramesh K. Srivastava makes an apt observation on the novel in the following words:

> With the advantage of a German mother, a Bengali father and having lived both in Germany and in India, Anita Desai naturally feels at home in depicting scenes and characters both German and Indian with equal felicity. What is common for Baumgartner in Germany and in India are the same sort of violence, lawlessness, inhumanity, tyranny and fanaticism. By making Baumgartner experience the same sort of things in both the countries, Anita Desai lends to the novel a universal significance (*University News* 1994:119).

Her latest novel, *Fasting, Feasting* (1999) unfolds the story of a small family in which Mamand Papa are the central characters with three children. Desai writes: "MAMANDPAPA, Mama Papa, Papa Mama. It was hard to believe they had ever had separate existences, that they had been separate entities and not Mama Papa in one breath" (*Fasting*, *Feasting* 5).

Uma and Aruna, two daughters are shown as contrasts. Uma was cheated in her marriage and ultimately brought back home by her parents. Aruna, on the other hand got a good husband and moved to Bombay to lead a prosperous and happy life. The only son, Arun who was sent to U.S.A. for higher studies came back disappointed.

Anita Desai's insight into human nature, and portrayal of characters particularly women characters and above all, command of language make her novels immensely readable.

Nayantara Sahgal's *Rich Like Us* (1985), *Plans for Departure* (1985) and *Mistaken Identity* (1988) are novels about history, nationalism and above all, contemporary life. Sahgal won the Sahitya Akademi Award for *Rich Like Us* for the year 1986. This novel is written against the backdrop of Emergency declared in

1975. The political theme is implicit in it. Sonali Ranade, an I.A.S. Officer in the Ministry of Industries was punished with demotion as she refused to sanction a 'preposterous' foreign collaboration project. Sahgal depicts how all norms of life were flouted during Emergency. Political theme is only one aspect of the novel. I concur with M.K. Naik when he says,

> The other dominant theme is the presentation of different facets of feminine experience, both oriental and occidental. The Indian women suffer in different ways at the hands of men. Sonali sees the young Marxist she once loved while at Oxford dwindling into an ambitious bureaucrat who becomes a willing tool in the hands of politicians, until a fall from grace brings retribution and self-recognition. Mona, the wife of Ram and the mother of his only son, finds herself discarded when her husband brings home Rose, an English girl, as his second wife. Nishi, daughter of a middle-class shopkeeper watches helplessly as her good-for-nothing husband, who is the son of a prosperous businessman, allows his father's garment-business to go to ruins. And in the memoir of her grandfather, Sonali reads the gruesome account of how her great-grandmother was forced to commit *sati* by her relations after her husband's death.
>
> Of the Western women, Rose, who falls in love with Ram and comes away with him to India, even when she knows that he is already married and has a son, is disillusioned when she discovers the gulf between her own cockney, working-class ways and Ram's life of refinement and culture. In the end, she is murdered by her stepson, as his father is reduced to a vegetable existence after a paralytic stroke. Rose, the working-class woman is well contrasted with Marcella, the upper middle-class lady, who is Ram's next flame, while Minnie is the typical British colonial wife, and the picture of her set is pure Kipling.
>
> The two worlds of public events and private experience impinge constantly upon each other in the narrative, since Sonali, the protagonist acts and suffers in both and this endows the novel with a firm structural unity. The irony in the title is plain. The phrase, 'Rich like

> us' is used in the very first chapter by Neuman, who has business dealings with Ram. It voices the American belief that if only the Indians followed American ways, they would be 'rich like us' (14). But, in the end, Sonali, who decides to devote herself to a study of the seventeenth century in India, realizes that her country is rich in a far different way—rich in its cultural heritage and that 'immersed in the past,' she can at the same time and actually as a result of this, prepare for the future. It is reassuring for her to realize that "I was young and alive, with my own century stretched out before me, waiting to be lived" *(IL* 121, Sept.-Oct. 1987:30-31).

Plans for Departure examines Indo-British relationship in artistic terms and *Mistaken Identity* is about Bhushan Singh, who returned home unsuccessfully from U.S.A. These two novels are nowhere near *Rich Like Us* in social commitment and do not have much contemporary relevance.

Shashi Deshpande is one of the most accomplished women novelists of postmodern period. Her novels are titled *The Dark Holds No Terrors* (1980), *If I Die Today* (1982), *Come Up and Be Dead* (1983), *Roots and Shadows* (1983), *That Long Silence* (1988), *The Binding Vine* (1993) and *Small Remedies* (2000). She won the Sahitya Akademi Award for *That Long Silence* for the year 1990. This is one of the most outstanding novels in our time. The theme of *That Long Silence* is simple. Jaya, the heroine of the novel, recalls her married life with nostalgia. She was married to Mohan and lived with him at different places till he went away from her to clear himself of the charge of business malpractice. She bore him two children and the third child was aborted. She recalled her relationship with innumerable relatives and friends with compassion and understanding. She tried to come to terms with herself by trying to write about herself and her family and was determined to break a 'Long Silence.' The novel ends with the return of her son, Rahul, the promise of Mohan 'to return' on Friday morning and Jaya changing the idea of their marriage and learning the truth that 'Life has always to be made possible.' Behind this simple story of the novel lies the ground swell of frustration in married life of the protagonist, who failed to be closer to her husband mentally.

She suffered from isolation. Despite her marriage to Mohan and subsequently becoming a mother of two children, she was lonely. Her husband could not understand her feelings as a result of which she was torn from within. Shashi Deshpande uses a beautiful image to describe Jaya's married life:

> A pair of bullocks yoked together...a clever phrase, but can it substitute for the reality? A man and a woman married for seventeen years. A couple with two children. A family somewhat like the one caught and preserved for posterity by the advertising visuals I so loved. But the reality was only this. We were two persons. A man. A woman (8).

To an Indian reader the image of a pair of bullocks yoked together suggests a world of meanings. It means that the bullocks so yoked shared the burden between themselves but no one knows whether they love each other or not. The image of the beasts performing the duty mechanically undermines the husband-wife relationship, who are united in marriage for love and not for leading a mechanical life terminating in mutual hatred and distrust. Jaya resents the role assigned to a wife in our country, who is called upon to stay at home, look after the babies and keep out of the rest of the world. She could not continue her writing as Mohan discouraged her. "I gave up my writing because of you," she said to Mohan. She was deeply distressed to know that the writer in her could not come to light because of her husband. She says:

> I had known then that it hadn't mattered to Mohan that I had written a good story, a story about a couple, a man who could not reach out to his wife except through her body. For Mohan it had mattered that people might think the couple was us, that the man him. To Mohan, I had been no writer, only as exhibitionist (144).

She did not take a risk to annoy Mohan lest that should break her marriage. She says ironically:

> Perhaps, if Mohan had been angry, if he had shouted and raged at me, if he had forbidden me to write, perhaps I would have fought him and gone on. But he had only shown me his hurt. And I had not been able to counter that. I had relinquished them instead, all

> those stories that had been taking shape to me because
> I had been scared—scared of hurting Mohan, scared to
> jeopardising the only career I had (144).

She was fed up with the routine work like changing the sheets, scrubbing bathrooms and cleaning the fridge, and so on.

That Long Silence depicts the plight of an educated Indian woman of our time. The significance of the novel depends on how far the reader is able to realize the situation and go along with the author in finding out the meaning. In a way, the protagonist, Jaya, is any modern woman who resents her husband's callousness and becomes the victim of circumstances. By implication the character of Jaya represents modern woman's ambivalent attitude to married life. Shashi Deshpande hints at the modern woman's refusal to comply with the wishes of the husband. The reader is free to interpret the heroine as a woman who failed her husband or otherwise. Alternatively, he may also take her as a representative woman of the contemporary society who is all set to revolt against the husband. Jaya is both an individual and a type, and the reader is free to take her in any manner he likes.

Shobha De is known for her erotic novels. Erotica apart, her novels have immense literary values in terms of the experimentation in the use of language and creation of an Indian English idiom. Two of her novels, *Sisters* (1992) and *Snapshots* have contemporary relevance.

The theme of sisters makes an interesting reading. Mikki (Mallika), the protagonist returned home following the deaths of her parents in an air-crash. Seth Hiralal and his wife (Mikki's parents) were survived by their only daughter and heir to their vast property. Mikki returned home and oversaw their funeral and took charge of Hiralal Industries. Seth Hiralal had sired another daughter, named Alisha by his concubine, Leelaben. This secret was known to Ramanbhai, a trusted employee of the Seth. Alisha was splitting venom on Mikki for not being able to get the social sanction as Seth's daughter. She was outraged by the obituary column that Seth was "Survived by his only child, a daughter, Mallika, studying in the US" and decided to take on the stepsister one day. Ramanbhai was running with the deer and haunting with the hound by trying to be closer both to

Mikki and Alisha. He had an axe to grind. Being an educated and liberated young women without any legitimate guardian to look after her, Mikki attended many parties and came in contact with many young as well as not so young persons. Many young men were interested in her. Navin, her friend, Shanay, her distant relative (Anjanaben's son) and industrialist, Binny Malhotra were interested in her. After rejecting Shanay, Mikki got engaged to Navin. Binny made all tricks possible to win over her. As ill luck would have it the precarious financial position drove Mikki to ask for a loan from Navin before marriage. Navin's mother turned it down and Mikki reacted quickly by breaking the engagement. Binny took advantage of the situation and lured away Mikki by giving costly presents and promising financial help. Binny being an elderly person and a past master in the art of love making lured Mikki to his bed and forced her to marry him. Mikki married him much against the wishes of her well-wishers and came to grief soon. Binny showed his true colour after marriage and Mikki willy-nilly became a domestic woman. Binny continued to sleep with women of his choice and Mikki got the shock of her life to know that he had a concubine named Urmi and two children by her—a son and a daughter. Mikki was beaten and forced to leave the house by Binny. She came back to her parents' place and decided to take Alisha's help. Alisha was in no mood to oblige her. Alisha like Mikki was a free bird. She had affairs with Navin and Dr. Kurien. She was almost dead when she attempted suicide but was luckily survived by the nourishment of Dr. Kurien and Mikki, who gave blood for her. This incident brought them closer, and they stayed together. Binny died in a road accident and Mikki felt very sad. She again became the owner of her property as well as the property of her late husband. Ramanbhai planned her murder, but she was saved by Shanay. Alisha took her to Geneva and got her cured. Two sisters understood each other, and love triumphed over hate as they decided to marry and set their house in order.

The best of passage in the book which almost brings to our mind the famous description of the touching scene of the Queen's death by Lytton Strachey in his book *Queen Victoria*, is Mikki's reaction to Binny's death and funeral. It is one of the best passages ever written by any Indian English novelist of our time. Mikki slowly begins to realise life as if she sees it in a mirror and with controlled passion and subdued grief, she feels the power of love that wins always. Shobha De writes:

> "Mikki couldn't wait to get out of that place. She was booked on the evening flight. As she looked at the largest coffin, she imagined Binny lying inside with a sneer on his face, laughing at the grotesquerie of life, laughing at her. She suppressed the desire to join in his laughter. She thought of happier times and her expression automatically softened. Suddenly it dawned on her that she didn't resent anything about him at all. Not even his brutality towards her. Perhaps that's what they call 'true love,' she thought wryly, a soft smile on her face. She looked at the other coffins and found herself feeling strangely happy for Urmi and her children. They were all together at last. Something they couldn't be when they were alive. Mikki shut her eyes and fell into a light reverie induced by the heady smell of spider lilies, roses and incense combined with the insistent beat of tiny cymbals as the priest droned on.... Mikki had a beautiful vision of Binny, dressed in his sharpest suit, ascending heavenwards, floating up like he was in a gently rising hot-air balloon. He was acknowledging the crowd gathered for his funeral with a jaunty wave of his hand, his lips twisted...she thought she saw his family—his real family—Urmi and her kids, floating happily around him, also waving and showering flower petals on everybody. Mikki felt a few descend on her shoulder...and then she jerked out of her trance as she realised the coffins were being lifted up and the people had begun throwing rose petals at the departing procession. Mikki watched as the men moved gracefully away, their white *kurtas* and *dhotis* standing out starkly against the bright green of the grass. It was just too beautiful. And she was glad to Binny. He would have approved...." (*Ibidem*: 174-75)

Shobha De's use of language and creation of new idioms by acclimatizing idioms from Indian languages to English language, adds to the charm of the novel. The narrative holds our breath for sensuous opulence and subtlety of variation and the result is that the novel becomes a 'best seller.'

Snapshots (1995) is about six women who belong to the upper class society. The blurb of the book unfolds the story:

> As the wine and conversation begin to flow at a reunion between six women, who were friends at school, memories start to surface—some happy, others bitter sweet and a few that are downright poisonous.... Forced to confront dark secrets that they thought lay buried deep in the past, the women begin to turn against one another, and the mood of the party turns nightmarish....

The world of *Snapshots* is a world of women where women begin to look at things from their point of view. They literally and metaphorically play with men and sometimes are played with by men. The novel depicts the love-play between men and women in great details. 'Morality' is a dirty word for the characters in the novel, for they believe in enjoyment of life, throwing the norms of the society out of window.

Six school mates—Aparna, Swati, Reema, Surekha, Rashmi and Noor—assemble at Reema's house on the occasion of Swati's return from the States. They go down the memory lane and ruminate over the past escapades. The theme of the novel makes an interesting reading. Swati wants her old friends to assemble in Reema's house years after they left their school and college. She tells Aparna plainly: "Why can't you just accept that I wanted to meet everybody? No tricks, no motives. It's been years. Besides, if I'd phoned just you, you wouldn't have come. Admit it. The truth is I organized this tamasha only to be able to meet you again" (181).

The novel begins with Aparna's going to Goa with Prem for a holiday. After they make love. Aparna remembers her ex-husband, Rohit and feels the difference. She gets a letter from Reema asking her to come to her (the latter's) house. Surekha, Rashmi and Noor are also invited to meet Swati. Since they are going to meet after years, Swati suggests that they should "bring Snapshots. Albums, Old Photographs, New Photographs, Mementos of their innocent past" (13). They all talk freely about their past as well as present love-affairs—pre-and post-marital relationships with men of their choice.

Within the framework of her novels, Shobha De depicts the breaking up of the institution of marriage. The new concept of marriage envisages complete sexual freedom with no notion of fidelity. In such a situation men and women merely become partners in love. Economic freedom, promiscuity and uncontrolled passion resulting from 'the lust of the blood' make most men and women vulnerable and the resultant frustration in life engulfs them. Shobha De presents love, sex and quarrels within the ambit of fictional framework. Life is presented as it is, not as it should be. De's use of language and her creation of a new idiom by acclimatizing the contemporary society to the English language, adds to the charm of the novel. What is important in De's novels is not their unconventional theme but an unusual treatment of sensual opulence in an intimate conversational language.

Arundhati Roy created history by Winning Booker Prize for her novel *The God of Small Things* for the year 1997. She is the first Indian English novelist to win this coveted award (I don't consider Rushdie as an Indian English writer, he is only of Indian origin and can best be described as Anglo-American Indian writer, if such a nomenclature is at all possible). Since her novel has been acclaimed as an outstanding novel in the whole range of Indian English fiction, I would like to make an elaborate discussion of it in an objective manner.

The plot of the novel is complex, and it moves both ways—backward and forward—and thereby makes the narration difficult and complicated. Thematically it centres round Ammu, her two children Raphel and Esthappen, her parents, brother, Chacko and his wife, Margaret and daughter, Sophie Mol and above all, Amu's low caste lover, Velutha, the paravan. The novel opens with Raphel's coming back to Ayemenem after a failed marriage, to see Estha, her twin brother ('they were two-egg twins,' 'dizygotic') who was sent to his father after Sophie Mol's funeral and now returned to their native place after twenty-three years. The whole family has been personalized in retrospection. The twins (Estha and Raphel) lived with their divorced mother, Ammu and their blind maternal grandmother, Mammachy and their maternal uncle Chacko, once a Rhodes scholar at Oxford and lecturer in Madras Christian College, who helped his mother to run their paradise pickle business, and their maternal grandfather's youngest sister, Baby Kochamma. Chacko was married to an English Woman, Margaret (who divorced him and married Joe) and had a daughter, Sophie Mol who died later by drowning.

Ammu's love for Velutha forms the core of the novel and makes the novelist's preference crystal clear. The traditional society was not only conservative but authoritarian for it laid down who should love whom. It happened long ago, and it is against this concept that the novelist protests vehemently. The right to love a man of her choice, is a woman's birth right and it should not be scuttled in the name of religion, caste, colour and class. It is in this sense that the novel could be read as a feminist novel or a post-colonial novel for both feminism and post-colonialism aim at destroying the old power structure. Roy wants to break this age-old tradition to uphold the right of a woman to marry a man of her choice. Thus, she says:

> ...it could be argued that it actually began thousands of years ago. Long before the Marxists came. Before the British took Malabar, before the Dutch Ascendancy, before Vasco da Gama arrived, before the Zamorin's conquest of Calicut. Before three purple-robed Syrian Bishops murdered by the Portuguese were found floating in the sea, with coiled sea serpents riding on their chests and oysters knotted in their tangled beards. It could be argued that it began long before Christianity arrived in a boat and seeped into Kerala like tea from a tea bag.
>
> That it really began in the days when the Love laws were made. The laws that lay down who should be loved, and how.

And how much (1997: 33).

'Things can change in a day' is used as a kind of refrain in the novel. It suggests that Roy is determined to break the tradition.

Who's The God of Small Things? Is it Velutha, the paravan, the maker of fine things with his superb sense of detail? Who could be have been? We are told:

> The God of Loss? The God of Small Things? The God of Goose Bumps and Sudden Smiles? Of Sour metal Smells

> like steel bus-rails and the smell of the bus conductor's hands from holding them? *(Ibidem* 217).

As if in a dream sequence, Ammu went with a cheerful man who had only one arm and could do only one thing at a time. "If he held her, he could not kiss her. If he kissed her, he could not see her. If he saw her, he could not feel her."

The liberation from old bondage and tradition needs not only courage but a new language. Arundhati Roy describes Ammu's (a high caste Syrian Christian woman) love for Valutha, (a Paravan, a low caste man) in poetic prose.

> She went to him and laid the length of her body against his. He just stood there. He didn't touch her. He was shivering. Partly with cold. Partly terror. Partly aching desire. Despite his fear his body was prepared to take the bait. It wanted her. Urgently, his wetness wet her. She put her arms around him.
>
> He tried to be rational: What's the worst thing that can happen?
>
> I could lose everything. My job. My family. My livelihood. Everything.
>
> she could hear the wild hammering of his heart.
>
> She held him till it calmed down. Somewhat.
>
> She unbuttoned her shirt. They stood their skin to skin. Her brownness against his blackness. Her softness against his hardness. Her nut-brown breast (that wouldn't support a toothbrush) against his smooth ebony chest. She smelled the river on him. His particular Paravan smell that so disgusted Baby Kochamma. Ammu put out her tongue and tasted it, in the hollow of his throat. On the lobe of his ear. She pulled his head down towards her and kissed his mouth. A cloudy kiss. A kiss that demanded a kiss-back. He kissed her back. First cautiously. Then urgently. Slowly his arms came up behind her. He stroked her back. Very gently. She could feel the skin on his palms. Rough, Calloused. Sandpaper. He was careful not to hurt her. She could feel how soft she felt to him. She could feel herself through him. Her skin. The way her body existed only where he touched her. The rest of her was smoke. She felt him

> shudder against her. His hands were on her haunches (that could support a whole array of toothbrushes), pulling her hips against his, to let her know how much he wanted her *(Ibidem* 334-5).

Arundhati Roy fashioned a new language for fiction. Her use of language reminds us of Eliot's use of language in *Rock Choruses* and *Four Quartets.* Take for instance, Ammu's parting from Velutha after the consummation of love. Roy writes:

> "She moved closer, wanting to be within him, to touch more of him. He gathered her into the cave of his body. A breeze lifted off the river and cooled their warm bodies.
> It was a little cold. A little wet. A little quiet.
> The Air.
> But what was there to say?
> An hour later Ammu disengaged herself gently.
> 'I have to go.'
> He said nothing, didn't move. He watched her dress.
> Only one thing mattered how. They knew that it was all they could ask of each other. The only thing. Ever. They both knew that. Even later, on the thirteen nights that followed this one, instinctively they stuck to the Small Things. The Big Things ever lurked inside. They knew that there was nowhere for them to go. They had nothing. No future. So they stuck to the small things" (*Ibidem* 338).

The above quoted passage also explains the title of the novel.

While trying to give a historical perspective to Estha and Raphel, Chacko says:

> We're Prisoners of War. Our dreams have been doctored. We belong nowhere. We sail unanchored on troubled seas. We may never be allowed ashore. Our sorrows will never be sad enough. Our joys never happy enough. Our dreams never big enough. Our lives never important enough to matter" *(Ibidem* 53).

This kind of prose at once gives a made in India stamp to Indian English novel.

But the novel is not without blemish. In her attempt to describe love and sex freely she writes a few passages which border on pornography. The behaviour of the Police Station is a case in point.

'If I were you,' he said, 'I'd go home quietly.' Then he tapped her breasts with his baton. Gently. Tap, tap. As though he was choosing mangoes from a basket. Pointing out the ones that he wanted packed and delivered. Inspector Thomas Mathew seemed to know whom he could pick on and whom he couldn't. Policemen have that instinct *(Ibidem* 8).

In an ironic undertone Roy says:

> Behind him a red and blue board said:
>
> Politeness
> Obedience
> Loyalty
> Intelligence
> Courtesy
> Efficiency *(Ibidem).*

The chapter 'Abhilash Talkies' reads like a Shobha De novel. One wishes Roy should have revised this chapter (she says that she had not revised a single word while writing this novel). In the closing chapter some of the passages border on pornography. Here is one such passage:

> Ammu, naked now, crouched over Velutha, her mouth on his. He drew her hair around them like a tent. Like her children did when they wanted to exclude the outside world. She slid further down, introducing herself to the rest of him. His neck. His nipples. His chocolate stomach. She stippled the last of the river from the hollow of his navel. She pressed the heat of his erection against her eyelids. She tasted him, salty, in her mouth. He sat up and drew her back to him. She felt his belly tighten under her, hard as a board. She felt her wetness slipping on his skin. He took her nipple in his mouth and cradled her other breast in his callused palm. Velvet gloved in sandpaper *(Ibidem* 336).

Arundhati Roy can be credited with creating a new idiom and phrases like 'biological father,' 'dia-able age.' 'Sea-Secrets,' 're-Returned,' 'non-elect,' 'death coiled like an angry spring,' 'touchables,' 'Rice-Christians,' 'Clean children, like a packet of peppermints' 'as lonely as a wolf,' etc.

Besides, taking up cudgel for women's right to property and to choose their lovers, the novel also makes references to communist movement in Kerala and allusions to the

Mahabharata. This can be taken as a representative postcolonial novel for it seeks to restructure the power centre by giving right to women to live their lives in their own way, and fashions a new language for fiction by creating a new Indian English idiom.

Manju Kapur, an academic turned writer made a name with her first novel, *Difficult Daughters* (1998) winning the Best First Book Commonwealth writers prize for 1999. The plot of the novel is simple, and the story is fascinating. It is the story of a woman, Virmati who was hooked on with her Professor, Harish at the latter's insistence. The eldest daughter of Suraj Prakash and Kasturi (the eldest of their eleven children), Virmati had an ambition to be highly educated. As chance would have it, she came in contact with Professor Harish who came to stay in her aunt's house as a tenant.

The married Professor, Harish was not happy with his illiterate wife. He felt attracted towards Virmati and gradually came closer to her. Virmati though initially resisted his love (illicit love and passion), subsequently gave in. Their affair led to Virmati's refusal to marry Inderjit, an engineer, arranged by her family and then to abortion, while she was still in the college. The whole family turned against her, and she went through harrowing experiences. Finally, the Professor took her home as his second wife. Virmati, won the love of the Professor but lost both the families. Then came the partition and they moved to Delhi and Ida, a daughter was born. The novel here almost comes to an end except the epilogue. In the epilogue, we are told about Ida, who like her mother made a disastrous marriage and was divorced. She was 'husbandless, childless.' Both Harish and Virmati passed away. The novel begins with the death of Virmati and her cremation and the story is unfolded to us by Ida, her daughter who learnt all about her mother's past from her aunt. The novel begins with an assertion by Ida, "The one thing I had wanted was hot to be like my mother" and ends with her request to the dead mother "Do not haunt me anymore."

Apart from the novelists mentioned above quite a few novelists (both old and new) published their novels after 1980. These include, Chaman Nahal's (winner of Sahitya Akademi Award for *Azadi* for the year 1977), *The Triumph of the Tricolour* (1993),

P.V. Narasimhaiah's (former Primer Minister of India) *The Insider* (1988), Manoj Das' *Cyclones,* Raj Gill's Jo *Bole* (1983), Gautam Bhatia's *Short History of Everything* (1998), Raj Kamal Jha's *The Blue Bed Spread* (1999), Vikram A Chandra's *The Srinagar Conspiracy* (2000), Jamyang Norbu's *The Mandala of Sherlock Holmes* (1999), Pankaj Mishra's *The Romantics,* R.K. Laxman's *The Messenger* (1993), R.W. Desai's *Frailty, Thy Name is Woman* (1993), Jai Nimbkar's, *Come Rain* (1993), Radhika Jha's *Smell* (1999), Esther David's *The Walled City* (1997) and Sagarika Ghose's *The Gin Drinkers* (2000).

Postmodern Indian English fiction has a very luxuriant growth with nearly a hundred novels written by Indian English novelists and writers of Indian diaspora. (Since diasporic writers are not within the purview of my book, I have excluded them). Post-1980 Indian English fiction is postmodern and post-colonial fiction with a new exuberance of language resulting in the creation of an Indian English idiom, and its emphasis on history and myths of the land, and above all, sexual frankness. References to history as we find in Kiran Nagarkar's *Cuckold,* to myths as in Shashi Tharoor's *The Great Indian Novel,* to imperialist design as in Amitav Ghosh's *The Glass Palace* and to sexual frankness as in Arundhari Roy's *The God of Small Things* and Manju Kapur's *Difficult Daughters* are new modes of writing in Indian English fiction. Contemporary reality and political scenario attract the novelists without end. Love, sex, and life in the present context are depicted with objectivity and as a result the texts become 'worldly'. In fact, postmodern novels are written keeping in mind the elite audience both at home and abroad. To use Edward Said's terminology we can say that postmodern novels are 'in the world and about the world, hence, worldly.'

To conclude, I should say that Indian English fiction has brought revolution in the whole range of Indian English literature in the choice of subjects and language of expression. Its portrayal of characters is appropriate to the situation. Thus, Indian English fiction re-creates contemporary society with insight and justness. Therein lies the merit of Indian English Fiction.

Works Cited

Adhikari, M. "Female Empowerment in Amitav Ghosh's *The Calcutta Chromosome.*" *Indian Fiction of Nineties.* Ed. R.S. Pathak. New Delhi: Creative Books, 1997.

Amur, G.S. "A New Parable: Arun Joshi's *The City and The River.*" *Indian Literature* 144, July-Aug. 1991.

Chandra, Vikram. *Red Earth and Pouring Rain.* New Delhi: Penguin Books, 1995.

Carey, John. *The Sunday Times* 2 April 1999.

De, Shobha. *Sisters.* New Delhi: Penguin Books. 1992.

——. *Snapshots.* New Delhi: Penguin Books, 1995.

Deshpande, Shashi. *That Long Silence.* New Delhi: Penguin India, 1989.

Devy, G.N. "The Indian English Novel 1980-90: An Overview." *Indian English Fiction 1980-90: An Assessment.* Ed. Nilufer E. Bharacha and Vilas Sarang. New Delhi: B.R. Publishing Corporation, 1994.

Ghosh, Amitav. *The Glass Palace.* New Delhi: Ravi Dayal Publisher and Permanent Black, 2000.

Jon Mee. "After Midnight: The Indian Novel in English of the 80s and 90s." *Rethinking Indian English Literature.* Ed. U.M. Nanavati and Prafulla C. Kar. New Delhi: Pencraft International, 2000.

Kapur, Manju. *Difficult Daughters.* New Delhi: Penguin Books, 1998.

Nagarkar, Kiran. *Cuckold.* New Delhi: Harper Collins Publishers, 1997.

Naik, M.K. *Rich Like Us. Indian Literature* 121. Sept-Oct. 1987.

——and Shyamala A. Narayan. *Indian English Literature 1980-1990: Critical Survey.* New Delhi: Pencraft International, 2001.

Roy, Arundhati. *The God of Small Things.* New Delhi: India Ink, 1997.

Sabbu, Saraswati. "Shiv K. Kumar: An Interview." *Journal of South Asian Literature* 25:2,1990.

Sengupta, S. "In an Antique Land and Historicity in Fiction: A Post-colonial Attitude." *Indian Fiction of the Nineties.* Ed. R.S. Pathak. New Delhi: Creative Books, 1997.

Seth, Vikram. *An Equal Music.* New Delhi: Penguin India, 1999.

Srivastava, Ramesh K. "Anita Desai's 'Baumgartner's Bombay' A Study." *University News.* Feb. 7,1994.

Walsh, William. *Indian Literature in English.* London: Longman, 1990.

4

Postmodern Indian English Short Story

Though Indian English Short Story owes its origin to Kamala Sathianandan's *Stories from Indian Christian Life* published in 1898, the real beginning of this genre was made in the 1930s in the hands of Mulk Raj Anand, R.K. Narayan, and Raja Rao. It is a coincidence of literary history that the great-trio, Anand, Narayan and Rao are the pioneers of novel and Short Story in Indian English literature in the fourth decade of the twentieth century. If the western masters like Maupassant, Frank O' Connor, Theodore Powys influenced Mulk Raj Anand, R.K. Narayan was influenced by Chekhov and Raja Rao took the French masters as his guide and source of inspiration. But at the same time these great writers have not forgotten their roots. They search for their themes in Indian myths, epics, folk tales and an ancient tales. Shiv K. Kumar gives an account of the origin of Indian English Short Story in the following words:

> Although the Indian Short Story in English is comparatively a recent phenomenon, its genesis may be traced back to the ancient fables of the sixth century A.D. Its origin lies in such ancient classics as the Katha-Sarit-Sangara, Yogavashishtha, Brihat-Katha or the Panchtantra. As stories, these fables and tales were tightly structured and ingeniously conceived, although their primary objective invariably was didactic—geared more to instruct than to entertain their readers (1992: 9).

Between nineteen thirties and eighties we have a number of Indian English Short Story writers who have enriched this genre and made it popular among the readers. The names of the Indian English Short Story writers, who wrote from 1930s to 1980s include Mulk Raj Anand, R.K. Narayan, Raja Rao, K.A. Abbas, Khushwant Singh, Anita Desai, Manoj Das, Ruskin Bond, Sunita Jain, Kamala Das, Keki N. Daruwalla, Jayanta Mahapatra and a few others. In the postmodern period most of these writers have also contributed immensely to the growth and development of Indian English short story. New writers like Shashi Deshpande, Vikram Chandra, Shiv K. Kumar, and a few others have made their presence felt in this genre in the last two decades of the twentieth century. Before discussing all these writers individually, it is imperative on my part to analyse the trends in recent Indian English Short Story.

Indian English Short Story holds mirror unto contemporary society in our time *(i.e.,* in the post-1980 period). Stories are being written on various aspects of life and society such as love, death, attitude to women, corruption in public life, human relationship, and above all, superstitions and rituals that are prevalent in the society. The change in our society in terms of urbanisation and industrialisation becomes a favourite theme with our writers. Some stories are rooted in our tradition and culture. Animals also form a part of our Short Story as is evident in the works of Manoj Das and Ruskin Bond.

Myths play a vital role in the plot construction and stories are built around them. R.K. Narayan, Manoj Das, and a few others have employed national myths in their stories. Myths give a didactic touch to the themes. Along with myths, the short story writers also use anecdotes to give moral and philosophical touch to their stories. Superstitions in the society attract the attention of the writers. Beautiful stories like Khushwant Singh's "The Mark of Vishnu" are written on this theme. Fantasy, folk beliefs and ghosts are employed as themes in their stories. To read the ghost stories, particularly the stories of Manoj Das and Ruskin Bond is to transport oneself into an imaginary world, where supernatural elements have a great sway over human life. The stories about ghosts have a great charm and appeal for the readers. Vikram Chandra's *Love and Longing in Bombay* is an interesting story about the supernatural world.

In the postmodern period a good deal of stories have autobiographical elements in them as in the case of Ruskin Bond and Shiv K. Kumar. Some of the stories have also psychological insights into human nature. The horizon of Indian English short story has been broadened by the post- 1980 short story writers, who have taken as it were, 'all province' as their themes. Shiv K. Kumar made an interesting comment on the state of Short Story in the following words:

> If the short story in English remained subdued till the first quarter of this century, it has catapulted into a popular literary genre in the mid-eighties—thanks to the patronage of Doordarshan with its millions of viewers. This new medium is now treating its mammoth audience to dramatization of stories by our celebrated writers like R.K. Narayan (now known for his 'Malgudi Days') and Satyajit Ray. Such programmes as 'Ek Kahani'—and 'Katha Sagar' which has offered us ingenious adaptations of world classics—have encouraged our new writers to take to the short story as an exciting form of writing (1992:16).

Having said so, let me turn to individual writers who have contributed significantly to this genre in the postmodern period. Let me begin with the great-trio, Mulk Raj Anand, R.K. Narayan and Raja Rao who have published significant volumes of stories in recent years. As M.K. Naik and Shyamala A. Narayan have rightly observed:

> Collections of short stories by the older writers continue to appear, but some of them pose bibliographical problems, in that they are either old collections appearing under new titles, or a mixture of material already published years ago and new. This is specially true of both Mulk Raj Anand and R.K. Narayan. Anand's *Things Have a Way of Working Out* (1998) and *Tales Told by an Idiot* (1999) are both old wine with new labels. The second collection is actually only a reprint of selected short stories of Mulk Raj Anand (1977) edited by M.K. Naik, under a new title (2001:116).

R.K. Narayan's new collection of stories include *Old and New* (1981), *Malgdudi Days* (1982) and *Under the Banyan Tree* (1985). Irony is the keynote of many of his stories.

Narayan criticises the attitude of the political leaders to rename certain streets after the Indian leaders, in a significant story called "Lawley Road." In that story the Municipal Chairman wanted to uproot the statute of Sir Frederick Lawley without knowing anything about the man, and finally decided to install it once again. This is how Narayan makes a dig at the unwise decision of whimsical authorities:

> At the corner of Lawley Extension and Market there used to be a statute. People had got so used to it that they never bothered to ask whose it was or even to look up. It was generally used by the birds as a perch. The Chairman suddenly remembered that it was the statue of Sir Frederick Lawley. The Extension had been named after him. Now it was changed to Gandhi Nagar, and it seemed impossible to keep Lawley's statute there any longer. The Council unanimously resolved to remove it. The Council with the Chairman sallied forth triumphantly next morning and circumambulated the statute. They now realised their mistake. The statute towered twenty feet above them and seemed to arise from a pedestal of molten lead. In their imagination they had thought that a vigorous resolution would be enough to topple down the statue of this satrap, but now they found that it stood with the firmness of a mountain. They realized that Britain, when she was here, had attempted to raise herself on no mean foundation. But it made them only firmer in their resolve. If it was going to mean blasting up that part of the town for the purpose, they would do it. For they unearthed a lot of history about Sir Frederick Lawley. He was a combination of Attila, the Scourge of Europe, and Nadir Shah, with the craftiness of a Machiavelli (1983:101).

On learning that Frederick Lawley is a different person, who built Malgudie town, the Chairman of the Municipal Council decided to install the statue once again.

"The Chairman of Malgudi Municipality has been able to buy back as a present for the nation the statute of Sir Frederick Lawley. He proposed to install it in a newly acquired property which is shortly to be converted into a park. The Municipal Council have resolved that Kabir Lane shall be changed to Lawley Road" *(Ibidem* 105).

The undertone of irony is unmistakable. Similarly suspense is an important ingredient of some of Narayan's stories. In "An Astrologer's Day" Narayan describes the belief of our people in astrology and at the same time makes a dig at the so-called astrologers who hoodwink the people. In this story, the protagonist became an astrologer to avoid his arrest by the police for he thought that he had killed a villager. When he found the same person living, his joy knew no bounds. This is how R.K. Narayan depicts his character.

> He had a working analysis of mankind's troubles: marriage, money and the tangles of human ties. Long practise had sharpened his perception. Within five minutes he understood what was wrong. He charged three pies per question and never opened his mouth till the other had spoken for at least ten minutes, which provided him enough stuff for a dozen answers and advices. When he told the person before him, gazing at his palm, "In many ways you are not getting the fullest results for your efforts," nine out of ten were disposed to agree with him. Or he questioned: "Is there any woman in your family, may be even a distant relative, who is not well disposed towards you?" Or he gave an analysis of character: "Most of your troubles are due to your nature. How can you be otherwise with Saturn where he is? You have an impetuous nature and a rough exterior." This endeared him to their hearts immediately, for even the mildest of us loves to think that he has a forbidding exterior *(Ibidem* 4).

The ending unveils the suspense of the story, when the astrologer confessed before his wife why he ran away from his village and turned an astrologer.

> After dinner, sitting on the pyol, he told her, "Do you know a great load is gone from me today? I thought I had the blood of a man on my hands all these years. That was the reason why I ran away from home, settled here and married you. He is alive."
>
> She gasped. "You tried to kill!"
>
> "Yes, in our village, when I was a silly youngster. We drank, gambled and quarrelled badly one day—why think of it now? Time to sleep, he said, yawning, and stretched himself on the *pyol*" *(Ibidem* 7).

R.K. Narayan once told how he wrote stories and how the materials available in our country are sufficient to write any number of stories.

> At the end of every novel I have vowed never to write another one—a propitious moment to attempt a short or two. I enjoy writing a short story. Unlike the novel, which emerges from relevant, minutely worked-out detail, the short story can be brought into existence through a mere suggestion of detail, the focus being kept on a central idea of climax.
>
> The material available to a story writer in India is limitless. Within a broad climate of inherited culture there are endless variations: every individual differs from every other individual, not only economically, but in outlook, habits and day-to-day philosophy. It is stimulating to live in a society that is not standardised or mechanised, and is free from monotony. Under such conditions the writer has only to look out of the window to pick up a character (and thereby a story) (*Ibidem* VIII-IX).

Raja Rao published his third collection of stories, containing nine stories titled *On the Ganga Ghat* (1989) eleven years after his well-known collection, *The Policeman and the Rose* (1978), and suggested in the preface that, 'the whole book should be read as a single novel.' But the author's idea of reading the collection as an integral story seems to have been belied. M.K. Naik and Shyamala A. Narayan are right in saying that:

> These character sketches cannot be said to rank with Raja Rao's earlier creations like "Javni," "Akkayya" and "Narsiga" in which he drew upon his own early experience of the Karnataka social scene. The Benares sketches, on the other hand clearly betray the hand of the outsider-observer. Nor does *On the Ganga Ghat* have anything comparable to the profound metaphysical parables in *The Policeman and the Rose*. The last piece of Ganga and Benares is full of metaphysical musings, so typical of Raja Rao. But there is no attempt to transmute it into a viable narrative as in earlier stories like "India, A Fable" and "The Policeman and the Rose." This may lead one to suspect that far from being a recent creation. On the *Ganga Ghat* is possibly a gathering of stray, early chips from the Raja

> Rao workshop, slightly shop-soiled, and visibly dated (2001:118).

K.A. Abbas, Khushwant Singh and Manohar Malgonkar, like the great trio Anand, Narayan and Raja Rao have published their collection of stories in between our independence and nineteen eighty and are well-known in our country. In the postmodern period they have published their new collections and brought out earlier published stories under new titles like the collected stories. K.A. Abbas' the new collection, *The Gun and Other Stories* (1985) contains thirteen stories on various themes ranging from film world to village. But these stories lack the spark of this earlier stories like "sparrows" and "sardarji."

Khushwant brought out his new volume, *The Collected Short Stories of Khushwant Singh* (1989) putting all his four collections published between 1950 and 1971. He has stated clearly in his foreword to this book what he values in a short story. According to him it should have a beginning, middle and an end, a "ring of truth," "a message to convey" and "sting in its tail." His sense of humour and dig at the ills of the society caused by superstition and corruption is well-known. His best-known story, 'The Mark of Vishnu' lays bare the superstition of the illiterate or semi-literate people of our country and therefore it has become a favourite story with the readers.

Manohar Malgonkar has published three volumes of stories between 1974 and 1977, and his fourth collection of stories titled, *Four Graves and Other Stories,* containing fifteen stories appeared in 1990. M.K. Naik and Shyamala A. Narayan made an interesting comment on this collection of stories in the following words:

> Seven of the fifteen stories here have already appeared in *Bombay Beware* (1975). The eight new stories have mostly a colonial colouring. The most interesting of these is perhaps the title story, "Four Graves," an ironic presentation of how myths are made. The graves of two dogs ("Mags" and "Sherkhan") of a British offer in time come to be respectively, a shrine of a Hindu deity (Mangesh) and a Muslim *pir*; and since the graves are side by side, it does not take long for communal trouble to erupt (*Ibidem* 118-9).

Some of our well-known poets like Jayanta Mahapatra, Shiv K. Kumar and Keki N. Daruwalla published their collection of stories in the postmodern period. Jayanta Mahapatra's *The Green Gardner* contains eighteen stories. His stories are different from the conventional stories in the sense that they focus not so much on the thematic content as on the subtlety of form and expression. Mahapatra explores many grey areas of human existence in the contemporary world and gives vent to the feelings of individuals in trying situations. What is important in his stories is the evocation of human agony in a dehumanized world. In 'The Mango Tree,' the tree planted by the husband becomes a symbol of life for the woman. She reflects:

> The Mango Tree, there in the yard beyond, looks in through my window into my life. There it stands, sharp- sighted and alert, pressing against the dark firm earth, its roots somewhere deep inside the darkness of the dead. It is not hard for me to imagine those roots-twisted, lonely exploring, turning away here and there, growing into silence, into the slime of both my past and my future. (93)

The tree for this woman is 'the centre of my (her) life' and it is her 'my mango tree.' But the members of the family fail to understand her sentimental attachment to this mango tree. That broke her heart. With a heavy heart and deep agony she asked:

> What have you done to my tree?
> Why have you cut it down (97).

The agony of an old man for being neglected in the family and ill-treated by his daughter-in-law, abides. In "Old Man in the Dark" Mahapatra depicts the plight of an Old man in such a subtle way that this 'old man' becomes all old men and the daughter-in-law becomes all daughters-in-law in this harsh world where purblind men enact hell. The old man bitterly complains:

> Everyone else comes first in this house. And it is I who am responsible for that husband of hers! Ungrateful Wretches (84).

Finally the harsh behaviour of the daughter-in-law compels the oldman to commit suicide.

Mahapatra probes deep into the dark recess of the human heart and sees not only the agony but the desire to gratify the senses. In "An Afternoon of Doctor Das" Doctor Das a sixty-two years old man (Sixty-two is a grandfather's age), deflowers a fifteen-year-old girl in a lonely afternoon. The story exposes the hypocrisy of the so-called civilised men who can be savage in their lonely moments.

Jealousy, poverty, greed and revenge motif can lead a man to force his wife into another man's arms, as we find in 'Turn left for Happiness.' Appa Rao, the rickshaw puller, driven by poverty and being suspicious of his wife, Malati's character and her relationship with liquor dealer, Kasi Biswal, forced her to sleep with another man for rupees thirty only. In another story, 'Ringing Silences,' a suspicious wife watches the telephone call of her husband. This situation was saved by the husband's reassuring tone 'I Love you too' in reply to her 'I love you.' She came to her senses and said, "What was wrong with me?" In 'Eyes' we get the picture of an anguished husband because of the failing eyesight of his wife.

> I looked at her then, now disappearing into the darkness behind a bank of cloud. Soon, very soon, she would not be able to see anything at all.... And looking at her then, I seemed to hear night-bird's cry: a place where time stood still, and hours sank into the horizon of pity (33-34).

"The Hotel Room" exposes the hollowness of the so-called modern sophisticated people who run away from their wives to gratify their lust in hotel rooms. In a highly emotional tone, Mahapatra describes a scene in poetic-prose in which a man and a woman make love in an act of deception and self-deception.

> Night, so very foetal, by itself beside a strange woman. I sacrifice my proverbial neutrality, even artistic ambitions. Far, far away I am a poet. She never knows who I am....
>
> This earth is you and I, assembled by black blood. Her name is Gina.... She tells it you glibly tonight's name. Tomorrow, who knows? (43).

In 'Red' we find how fear complex affects the characters of individuals. The protagonist's fear for the red eye of Habib Khan, makes him afraid of anything that looks red. Mahapatra's observation: "Each one's secrets are his or hers alone" seems to explain the protagonist's predicament of life. Habib Khan reflects:

> It led me to believe too that there could be nothing concrete between birth and dying, the wall of years totally meaningless (117).

Mahapatra's stories tell us about human condition and helplessness resulting in pain, agony and loneliness. The language is adequate to the thematic content and above all there is felicity of expression. There is a kind of poetic touch, that heightens the memorable and appeal of his stories. The stories of Mahapatra sing, for the rhythm of poetic-prose is highly commendable. It is an irony of fate that when most of his poems are prosaic, his prose is poetic. The short, crisp and thought-provoking sentences written in conversational and simple language attract the attention of the readers and make the stories interesting and lively. It seems that the poet in Mahapatra, never leaves Mahapatra, the story-teller. Like the endings of his poems, the ending of his stories (at least, most of it) is intricate but there are hints and guesses that 'whisper results.' His technique remains the same. So it will not be wrong to say that his stories are an extension of his poetry.

Shiv K. Kumar has published two collections of stories in recent years. The titles are *Beyond Love and Other Stories* (1980) and *To Nun with Love* (2001). Kumar dives deep into human psyche and recreates characters in their own situation. In a story called, "Mrs Williamson," Kumar depicts the protagonist, Mrs Williamson with an insight that is replete with a touch of pathos. She believes that she could send a message to her husband Chris who died ten years ago through some dying man. She thinks she could communicate with her. Kumar is essentially a romantic at heart. Most of his stories in both the collections stated above are about love and the characters in the stories are youngmen and women beaming with love and desire. "To Nun with Love" is about a youngman who fell in love with the Nun and the latter's reaction to it. The Nun being disgusted with the improper action of the youngman decided to make a confession and resign her job. It ends with the youngman's promise not to write a letter to her again. In a story titled, "Fingers," Kumar writes about the predicament of the lovers and their obsession with writing love letters. The poet in Kumar takes over from Kumar the story-teller, when the lover writes to the beloved the following words:

> I am in love with every part of your body. But, above all, with your delicate fingers, which burn in my heart all the time, like multicoloured scented candles. I imagine your fingers playing on my heartstrings, creating symphonies which are enthralling than the music of the spheres. This is my only antidote to the banality of my profession, selling tea to the public.
>
> I want to be with you, always and everywhere. I could renounce my religion and my family for your sake. I'd even run away with you, if you'd just nod your head (2002:129).

M.K. Naik and Shyamala A. Narayan made an interesting observation on Kumar's first collection of stories:

> The twenty-five stories in Shiv K. Kumar's *Beyond Love and Other Stories* (1980) show considerable variety of setting and character. The scene shifts from India to Bangladesh and also to USA, and the characters range from a flirtatious husband to a sanyasi, a soldier to a clergyman and a constant wife to a nun. Short, slick and readable, the stories are however, thin in content. Only occasionally, a story like, 'Beyond Love' stands out by its psychological interest. Here, a newly widowed young woman goes into a trance-like state, in which she mistakes her husband's best friend for her husband himself and drags the horrified man into her bed (2001: 121).

Keki N. Daruwalla published his second collection of stories titled, *The Minister for Permanent Unrest and Other Stories* in 1996. The 'locale' of his stories varies from state to state. M.K. Naik and Shyamala A. Narayan drew our attention to this aspect of Daruwalla's stories in the following words:

> Along with U.P., the Punjab, Kashmir and Assam, Arabia and Persia also provide the background. Among the characters are a *sufi* saint, a Persian poet, a Parsi girl eloping with a Muslim youth, and a Sikh boy in love with a Hindu girl. Perhaps Daruwalla's most achieved story is "The Potting of the White," an acute study of

> race relations during colonial days. But one wonders why the poet in Daruwalla almost never comes out in any of his narratives (2001:121).

Manoj Das and Ruskin Bond are the two most well-known Indian English short story writers after R.K. Narayan. Though they have written novels and novellas in English, they are primarily known as short story writers. It is a coincidence that both of them were born in the same year—that is 1934. Ruskin Bond is the only Indian English short story writer who has been honoured by the Central Sahitya Akademi with its annual award in 1992.

Manoj Das is a bilingual (should we say ambilingual?) short story writer. He writes both in English and Oriya. The originality in themes is matched by the felicity of expression in an idiom that is shared, by all the English-speaking Indians and above all, is intelligible to the English-speaking world outside India. His stories are deeply rooted in the native soil *i.e.* the birth place of the writer, in Orissa and they evoke the landscape of the place in unmistakable terms. Manoj Das' important collection of short stories include *The Crocodiles Lady* (1975), *Fables and Fantasies for Adults* (1978), *The Vengeance and Other Stories* (1980), *The Submerged Valley and Other Stories* (1986), *The Miracle and Other Stories* (1993), and *Farewell to Ghost* (1994). His stories dive deep into human psyche and present characters as they are, not as they should have been. Das exposes the characters who preach one thing and practice the other, by unmasking them. His characters are real persons whom we encounter in our daily life, only names have been changed. Let us take a story like, "Mystery of the Missing Cap." Two important characters here are Sri Moharana, a well-to-do villager who "nurtured an ambition to be elected to the State Legislature" and Babu Virkishore, Minister for Fisheries and Fine Arts. Virkishore was invited to the village by Moharana to create field for the latter's entry into the Legislature. Ministers are good at speech making. They advise people to practise simple living and high-thinking, but they do the reverse in their private life.

Irony is implicit in most of the stories of Das. In our society it has become a habit with the people of one profession to look down upon the people of another profession. In 'Encounters'

Das presents two characters, a school teacher and another chauffeur. The writer tells us that both of them were classmates and they used to sip tea in the same canteen after years of their schooling, they recognise each other but do not talk because each one thinks he is superior to the other.

Manoj Das' themes in short fiction are vast-ranging from ghosts, animals, humans to demons. His world is warm, palpable, and his characters are known by their chief intensity as the author himself. There are hints and guesses, pathos and humour, subdued irony and gentle mockery that go well with the plot and the situation. He never spares people of dubious nature and reputation. While dealing with contemporary situation, he comes down heavily on those who corrupt the society and hoodwink the public. Stories dealing with contemporary life and society where parents are cast away by children as in "Trespassers" or friends disown each other as in "Encounters" have atmosphere surcharged with subdued irony and the tone becomes potentially mocking. Although Das does not create another Malgudi like R.K. Narayan, the locale of most of his stories is the same, *i.e.* a small place in Balasore District of Orissa. The landscape of the place with a nostalgia for the writer's past comes alive in most of his stories.

Ruskin Bond projects a part of his personality into his stories to make them authentic and interesting. *Our Trees Still Grow in Dehra,* as the blurb of the book says, is "Semi-autobiographical in nature" and, therefore, can be read as a disguised autobiography.

In his opening remarks "Maplewood: An Introduction" Ruskin Bond harks back to the past, when he came to live in the Maplewood cottage, resigning his job in Delhi. He writes:

> It was all done on an impulse—the decision to give up my job in Delhi, find a cheap house in a hill-station, and return to freelance writing. It was a dream I'd had for sometime, lack of money had made it difficult to realize. But then, I knew that if I was going to wait for money to come, I might have to wait until I was old and grey and full of sleep. I was thirty-five—still young enough to take a few risks. If the dream was to become reality, this was the time to do something about it (1991:X).

Most of the stories of this collection, *Our Trees Still Grow in Debra* were written here. Ruskin Bond was rooted in the place and became a part of it. He states, "Once you have lived with mountains, there is no escape. You belong to them."

Love of nature and concern for ecological imbalance in the Hills, make the writer sad as he sees the felling of trees and the rapid deforestation going on all around him. In some of his stories he makes a dig at the unwise decision of the authorities to cut trees and build roads and buildings in their place. In "Death of the Trees," Bond tells us how the felling of trees one by one, had broken his heart. What pains him more is our lack of understanding of the importance of the trees to maintain ecological balance. He writes with a tinge of irony.

> The peace and quiet of the Maplewood hillside disappeared for ever one winter. The powers that be decided to build another new road into the mountains, and the PWD saw fit to take it right past the cottage, about six feet from the large window which had overlooked the forest (OTSGID, 1991:93).

On the surface level this story records the author's reaction to the felling of trees which makes the hill bare and forest birds homeless. 'Forest birds, all of them, they will now be in search of some other stretch of surviving forest. The only visitors will be the crows, who have learnt to live with, and off humans, and seem to multiply along with roads, houses and people,' says Bond with a deep sigh. Deforestation is closely followed by rapid urbanisation causing damage to the environment and creating ecological imbalance to the region. At the deep level, the author resents the mindless action of the power that be, in felling trees along the hillside. Bond concludes this story with an implicit warning: "Never mind. Men come and go; the mountains remain" (113-14).

Apart from the autobiographical elements, one notices a note of didacticism in the short stories of Ruskin Bond. The desire to teach and preach is unmistakable. "The Bent-Double Beggar" is replete with didacticism. Here are some of the teachings of the Bent-Double Beggar:

(i) "It is no use getting upset about delays in India: they come with unfailing punctuality."

(ii) "His favourite proverb: If you must eat dung, eat elephant's dung."

(iii) "One can forgive ignorance in a man who has had little or no education, but ignorance in a man who has been to college is unforgivable. Yet it is quite common."

(iv) "For democracy to succeed, the first requirement is that the majority of people should be honest."

(v) "Nietzsche was wrong; it isn't action but pleasure that binds us to existence."

"It is difficult to be miserable all the time. Human nature won't permit it. Even when we are burning or burying our dead, we are thinking of what we will eat or drink later in the day."

(vi) "Chance gives, and takes away, and gives again."

(vii) "I travelled a lot once (said Ganpat), but you can go on doing that and not get anywhere. Wherever you go or whatever you do, most of your life will have to happen in your mind. And there's no escape from that little room" (*Ibidem.* 22-23).

The above quotations remind us of Bacon's aphorism. It seems that Bond wants to preach through his stories. The moralising tone in his stories is unmistakable.

Ruskin Bond's stories reveal his love of nature and particularly his attachment to trees. They are firmly rooted in Dehra. The landscape of the place haunts him without end. Like Wordsworth's visit to Tintern Abbey, Bond's stay at Dehra helps him to build an intimate relationship with the hillside, trees, and birds, which becomes an integral part of his life. To live without them becomes painful for him. By doing violence to nature, man has caused ecological imbalance which ultimately harms him. Therefore, Bond warns mankind against this kind of violence to nature in a number of his stories. The rapid urbanisation and deforestation would spell disaster for mankind someday.

The Indian English short story writers like Dina Mehta, Kamala Das, Shashi Deshpande, Anita Desai, Sunita Jain and a few others have contributed immensely to that genre. I concur with Shiv K. Kumar when he says:

> Our women writers seem to have lent a new dimension of sensitivity and perception to the short story in English. They find its limited canvas quite congenial to their sensibilities in confronting their brief, often muted, experiences. They prefer to say a thing or two, and then let the rest fade away into silence. There's for instance, Dina Mehta, whose story 'Absolution' eddies around a fragile, almost veiled, emotion of jealousy. Nor does Nayantara Sahgal allow her protagonist in 'Martand' to speak out her heart. She just seems to flicker between her fidelity to her husband and an irrepressible heart-ache for the other man, the doctor, who is committed to alleviating human pain. There was that untouched innocence about Martand, a purity without which I could no longer live. That was why I couldn't give him up, however long we had to wait for this to work out. There was so little time to talk about personal problems, and when we were alone together, we did not talk. Indeed, the spoken word is such a futile instrument of communication in a woman's world—since it's often the language of knitted eyebrows, muted sighs, deep pauses and dazed looks that does it.
>
> That's the way most of our women writers tend to respond to reality with reticence, quietude and endurance. May be there's something masochistic about such an attitude, as is manifest in Sunita Jain's Story 'Heavy is Gold.' Here a young woman is married off to a widower 'twice her age' just for the sake of the yellow metal (1992:14).

Kamala Das stories before her poetry pale into insignificance. Her second collection of stories titled *Padmavati the Harlot and Other Stories* appeared in 1992, fifteen years after her first collection of stories, *A Doll for the Child Prostitute* (1977) was published. It reprints some of her earlier published stories. Love is the central and recurrent theme in her stories. The frankness with which she depicts love relationship between men and women is admirable.

Shashi Deshpande, a Sahitya Akademi Award winning writer for her novel, *That Long Silence* has a number of short story collections to her credit. Her stories first published in magazines like *Eve's Weekly, Femina, The Illustrated Weekly of India* and *Mirror* were later on collected in book form under the titles *The Legacy and Other Stories* (1971), *The Miracle and Other Stories* (1986), *It Was Dark* (1986) and *It was the Nightingale* (1986) and *The Intrusion and Other Stories* (1993). In her stories she recreates India in her present situation and the characters with authenticity and conviction. Deshpande articulates the feelings of middle-class women in quite a few of her stories. G.S. Balaram Gupta makes a valid point when he says:

> Shashi's women are conscious of their predicament: they are victims of inequity: they are creatures of conventional morality: they are the ones who are unfairly abused, misused and ill-used. But they believe in conformity and compromise for the sake on the retention of domestic harmony rather than revolt which might result in the disruption of familial concord. Shashi's fictional world is replete with only Savitris, not Noras (VJES I, 1993:39).

Some of her well-known stories are "The Inner Rooms," "The Awakening," "I want," "A Day Like Another," "Antidote to Boredom," "Intrusion" and "A Liberated Woman." "The Inner Rooms" depicts the predicament of the mythical character Amba who committed suicide out of frustration in life for her failure to marry the man of her choice. She could not marry Salva whom she loved because she was won by Bhishma for Vichitraveerya and the latter would not marry her because she loved Salva. Bhishma an avowed bachelor would not marry either. Thus the story depicts the plight of woman in a male dominated society. Again, the predicament of woman as wife is depicted in the stories like, "A Day Like Another," "Antidote to Boredom," and "Intrusion." I am inclined to quote Balaram Gupta again who makes apt observation on Deshpande's stories in the following words:

> Shash's stories are primarily woman-centred. Her thematic concerns are guilt, failure, loneliness—in brief, woman in her different roles, as wife, mother, daughter and as a human being in a society whose mores and conventions are rigidly conditioned by man. Shashi's women consciously suffer. They are "strong,

> full-bodied individuals with a mind of their own, with courage to face facts even about themselves and yet conforming to set patterns of life etched out for Indian women as identifiable as the wife next door." In other words, women in Shashi's fictional world are no doubt aware that they are victims of inequity, but they prefer suffering to rebellion and sacrifice to revolt in the interest of familial harmony. Shashi's stories reflect social reality as it is. She does not suggest how it ought to be. She gives no facile solutions.
>
> Shashi may not be startlingly technically innovative, but she is aware of the demands of the short story as an art form. Her characters and situations, kept to the irreducible minimum, are incisively sketched. Her recurrent use of first-person narration lends a ring of authenticity to her writing. She has no novelties to offer by way of experimentation with the language, but her English sounds simple and natural. Her style is lucid and direct, spontaneous and unpretentious, appropriate and adequate (*Ibidem* 40-41).

Anita Desai writes psychological stories by exploring the subconscious human mind. Twenty-two years after her first collection of stories, *Games at Twilight and Other Stories* (1978), she published her second collection titled *Diamond Dust* in 2000. If she presents the picture of a crude and greedy woman in "pineapple cake," in "private tuition" she depicts the plight of a poor teacher who is compelled by poverty to give private tuition to supplement his meagre income. Her stories are difficult because of her obsession with the exploration of the feminine mind and sensibility. She employs evocative images in her stories. She writes about the kind of life people live in India as well as in U.S.A.. M.K. Naik and Shyamala A. Narayan are forthright in expressing their views on Anita Desai's stories:

> The best story in *Diamond Dust,* "Winters cape," deals with the relationship between a young American girl and her Indian mothers-in-law. The women come all the way to America because they wish to help at the birth of their grandchild. They realise soon enough that they are a burden rather than a help to the American mother. The plight of the Indian man

> trying to bridge two worlds in depicted with feeling, though Desai introduces an unnecessary touch of the exotic by making him have two mothers, the biological mother who bore him and her sister who has brought him up, "Underground" is an unusual love story: the husband finds himself unable to welcome guests to his hotel after the death of his wife; instead, he spends his evenings feeding a family of badgers. In "The Artist's Life," a young schoolgirl finds her illusions about artists shattered when she observes the plight of the tenant living on their property.
>
> The stories set abroad are better than the Indian ones, which are quite without merit. Desai's recreation of the Indian scene seems to be based on memory. The descriptions are not completely false, it is more as if we are seeing things through a lens which is slightly out of focus. The unnecessary use of Indian words is another irritant. It may be a good strategy for Anita Desai to think twice before venturing to write about India any longer (2001:129).

Dina Mehta has two collections of stories, titled *The Other Woman and Other Stories* (1981) and *Miss Menon Did not Believe in Magic and Other Stories* (1994). His stories can be profitably studied as experiments in feminine sensibility jealousy is the primary emotion in her story, "Absolution." G.S. Balaram Gupta makes an opt comment on this story in the following words:

> "Absolution" is a pronouncedly feminist creation. Not satisfied with his continual acts of infidelity towards his "docile, chaste and devoted" wife Sita, Ram celebrates his lapses with triumphant glee by presenting her with varieties of flowers to mark them. When she is shocked into a recognition of her husband's perfidy. Sita retorts. She yields to the temptations posed by Ram's friend Dilip and bursts out of the cocoon of her "womanly faithfulness and days of long-suffering patience, all that disarming passivity" and presents her husband with a glowing bouquet of red carnations in "glad and chaotic abundance." The story emphatically questions the validity of conventional womanly virtues such as

> duty, chastity and submission in the context of man's violation of these values.
>
> The rest of Dina Mehta's stories offer variations on the same theme of man-woman relationships.
>
> Dina Mehta is more pronounced in her feministic stance than Shashi Deshpande. Her style is normally simple and spontaneous though at times she waxes Johnsonian. And she can vary her narrative strategy according to the thematic need of the story. Dina Mehta is sure to become a force to reckon with if she comes out with a few more volumes of stories/particularly stories like "Absolution" (VJES I 1993:42).

Sunita Jain and Raji Narasimhan, Lakshmi Kannan and Veera Sharma are some of our well-known Indian English short story writers. Sunita Jain's "Heavy is Gold" a young woman under compulsion agrees to marry a widower 'twice her age.' The agony of woman is depicted in artistic terms. Sunita Jain has two collections of stories titled, *A Woman is Dead and The Eunuch of Time and other Stories* to her credit. The betrayal of woman by man is a major theme in Jain's stories. Her women characters do not revolt. Her language is poetic and has great lyrical effect.

Indian English diasporic/expatriate writers like Jhumpa Lahiri, Bharati Mukherjee and Rohinton Mistry cannot be called Indian English writers. And hence, I have not included them here.

To conclude this chapter on Indian English short story, I should say that it has come up age. Both in theme and in technique, Indian English short story has broken new grounds. It can be favourably compared with short stories written in regional languages. The future of Indian English short story is immense.

Works Cited

Balaram Gupta, G.S. "Indian English Women Short Story Writer" *Vikram Journal of English Studies:* 1 (1993).

Bond, Ruskin. *Our Trees Still Grow in Dehra.* New Delhi: Penguin Books, 1997.

Kumar, Shiv K. Ed. *Contemporary Indian Literature in English.* New Delhi: Sahitya Akademi, 1991.

——. *Contemporary Indian Literature in English*. Shimla: Indian Institute of Advanced Studies, 1992.

——. *To Nun with Love and Other Stories*. Hyderabad: Orient Longman, 2002.

Naik, M.K. & Shyamala A. Narayan. *Indian English Literature 1980-2000: A Critical Survey.* Delhi: Pencraft International, 2001.

Narayan, R.K. *Malgudi Days*. New Delhi: Allied Publishers, 1983.

5

Postmodern Indian English Drama

Diachronically speaking Indian English drama is contemporaneous with Indian English poetry dating back to 1831 when K.N. Banerjee published the play titled, *The Persecuted or Dramatic Scenes Illustrative of the Present State of Hindu Society in Calcutta,* four years after Henry Derozio published his first book of verse called *Poems* in 1827. Thus, Indian English drama is older than Indian English novel, for the first novel in English by Bankim Chandra Chatterjee titled, *Raj Mohan's Wife* was published in 1864. And yet Indian English drama is nowhere in comparison either to Indian English poetry or fiction in recent years for various reasons. The second play in English titled, Is *This Called Civilization*? by Michael Madhusudan Dutt was published in 1871. As M.K. Naik has clearly stated that, "from 1831 to 1980, not less than 500 plays by Indian English writers had appeared, and during the short period of the last twenty years, about 75 have been published" (2001:201). The number is immaterial, for Indian English drama still suffers from neglect.

Three playwrights who have given a new direction to Indian English drama in the postmodern period are Girish Karnad, Nissim Ezekiel and Mahesh Dattani.

Girish Karnad like Manoj Das is a bilingual writer. He writes his plays first in Kannada and then renders them into English. This is not a case of translation but 'transcreation' (to use a happy term of P. Lal). Since Karnad himself renders his Kannada plays into English, they qualify to be a part of Indian English drama. This is what Manoj Das does while writing short stories first in Oriya and then rendering them into English and *vice versa*. It is interesting to recall here, Tagore's rendering of his Bengali play, *Raktakarabi* into English play, *Red Oleanders*. But the similarity with Karnad ends here, for Tagore's English play is considered to be inferior to his Bengali play, while Karnad's English versions of Kannada plays are better than the originals. That is because, Karnad's first language (L1) is Konkani and Kannada is his second language (L2). Karnad sought into prominence with the publication of his two plays *Tughlaq* in 1972 and *Hayavadana* in 1975. In the nineties he has written three more plays titled *Naga-Mandala* (1990), *Tale-Danda* (1993) and *The Fire and the Rain* (1998). All these plays are trans created into English by the playwright from Kannada originals and hence, qualify to belong to the canon of Indian English drama. M.K. Naik gives an interesting account of the origin of *Naga-Mandala* and the making of it out of two folk tales:

> In his preface to *Nagamandala,* Karnad says that the play is "based on two oral tales from Karnataka, which I first heard from Professor A.K. Ramanujan." He does not specify exactly which stories they are, but equivalent stories are found in practically every Indian language. The first is obviously the traditional tale of a cobra turning into man at night and visiting a married woman; and the second is based on the popular belief that a night long vigil in a temple can ward off death.

In the Prologue, a failed playwright is cursed with death, because he has sent so many people to sleep in the theatre; he is helped to stay awake by 'Story' personified, who recounts to him the exciting narrative of a Cobra and a married woman; newly-wed Rani is neglected by her husband, Appanna, who locks her up in the house; a King Cobra from an ant-hill nearby falls in love with her and starts visiting her at night in the form of her husband. When the husband comes to know this, Rani is ordered to prove her innocence by undergoing the 'Cobra Ordeal' *i.e.,* putting her hand into the ant-hill. She naturally emerges unscathed and is immediately hailed as a goddess by the village people. Finally, the Cobra finds shelter in the long tresses of Rani.

The two folktales are deftly blended in presenting the two allied themes of the nature of art and the relationship between art and imagination on the one hand and mundane reality on the other. The tale of the failed playwright seems to suggest that art demands everything from the artist and that he will die if he cannot fulfil his mission. The Rani-Appanna-Cobra tale is evidently an allegory of the nexus between the world of art and the world of mundane reality. Rani, who whiles away her time making up fairy tales is the artist, and the Cobra, the power of imagination, while Appanna represents the work-a-day world. The fact that the Cobra assumes the form of Appanna suggests that Art is, and also is not, the same as reality. That the Cobra finally finds permanent refuge in the hair of Rani is perhaps indicative of the permanent alliance between Art and Imagination.

"The play moves at a brisk pace, and the dialogue, which is in clear, simple everyday English without any conscious straining after 'Indianness,' suits the rustic folk-tale it presents as a surface structure, without causing harm to the deep structure of the symbolism beneath" *(Littcrit* 2001: 45-46).

In *Tale-danda* there is a conflict between religion and society. M.K. Naik outlines the theme of the play in the following words:

> The play deals with the final crisis in the life of Basavanna, the great social reformer in 12th century Karnatak, and the founder of the Lingayat faith. When he was chief minister at the court of King Bijjala of Kalyana, Basavanna tried to propagate his revolutionary philosophy the main tenets in which were: the abolition of caste; equality of the sexes; rejection of idol worship; repudiation of Brahminism, and of Sanskrit in favour of the mother tongue, *i.e.,* Kannada.
>
> The play shows how the higher castes resent Basavanna's iconoclasm, and how the resentment reaches its highest peak when one of Basavanna's Brahmin disciples gives his daughter in marriage to an untouchable. The culprits are severely punished, and in the subsequent holocaust, King Bijjala is dethroned by his orthodox son, while Basavanna dies in mysterious circumstances. (*Ibidem*)

In a discussion of Karnad's plays published in *Indian Literature* (Sept.-Oct. 1995) Prasanna, the well-known theatre director, U.R. Anantha Murthy, noted Kannada writer and Girish Karnad himself threw new lights on *Tale-danda:*

Prasanna: In *Tale-danda,* the brahmin mother voices her anxiety over her daughter marrying a *harijan*—'Oh my! My daughter vomits at the very smell of camphor, how can she ever manage in a Cobbler's household?'

When language and caste, occupation and caste, community and caste are interconnected, how do you give up one and retain the other? One can give up caste socially, but not culturally.

URA: That is Bijjala's question too. Basavanna answers; 'No barrier is true, you can transcend this.' 'That is *bhakti,* which enables you to transcend everything.

GK: There is this last scene in *Tale-danda* where Bijjala tries to grasp what is happening around through the eyes of a low-caste boy, who is sitting on his shoulders.... Bijjala wants to know whether Basavanna has come. What I wanted to achieve in this scene was exactly what you are trying to say; the notion of transcendence. The political significance of a boy from a lower-caste sitting on the shoulders of a king, is not as important to me as the idea that Bijjala is seeking. his liberation through this low-caste boy. For, what the boy sees and comments upon is important for Bijjala's liberation. It is important not just politically... (*Indian Literature:* 169, Sept.-Oct. 1995: 133-34).

The Fire and the Rain (1998) is based on a myth taken from the *Mahabharata.* This is clearly stated by the playwright in the *Preface:*

> The myth of Yavakri (or Yavakrita) occurs in Chapters 135-38 of the Vana Parva (Forest Canto) of the *Mahabharata.* It is narrated by the ascetic Lomasha to the Pandavas as they wander across the land during their exile. I have met Sanskrit scholars who were unaware of the existence of the myth; it is easy to lose track of a short narrative like this in the tangled undergrowth that covers the floor of that epic.

> I first came across the story of Yavakri and Paravasu, while still in college, in C. Rajagopalachari's abridgment of the *Mahabharata*. That Rajaji, confronted with the stupendous task of abridging the world's longest epic to about four hundred pages, should not have discarded this seemingly peripheral tale is a tribute to his sensitivity and judgment.
>
> It was fortunate for me that Rajaji did not do so, for the moment I read the tale, I knew it had to be turned into a play. For the next thirty-seven years, I struggled with it, trying to fit all the ramifications of the myth within some sort of a manageable shape (1998: IX).

D. Maya outlines the theme of the play in the following words:

> *The Fire and the Rain,* the latest and perhaps the most powerful of Karnad's play, is the reenactment of a puranic myth from the *Mahabharatha*—of Indra's destruction of his brother out of jealous fury. Arvasu's cry "why brother...? Why?" rings through the play voicing the puzzled fury and heart-rending agony of betrayal from a worshipped brother. The play has a complex framework with a central myth assuming the form of a dramatic performance within the larger framework of the story of Arvasu's betrayal by his brother Paravasu, the chief priest performing a yajna to bring rains to the drought-stricken land. Karnad uses the technique of iteration reinforcing the central theme through three parallel stories, each being an echo of stories of betrayal from time immemorial (*The Literary Criterion* 36: 4, 2001: 69).

The title of the play is symbolic. The "fire" is not the purgatorial fire but the "fire" of passion that leads to lust, revenge, violence and death. The "rain" on the other hand, symbolizes, regeneration, revival, life-giving, Divine Grace and forgiveness.

Nissim Ezekiel's *Don't Call It Suicide* (1993) is a tragedy in two Acts. It is based on a real life incident. Ezekiel's gives a clue to the background of the play in the following words:

> I was told about the event by an acquaintance of mine in an Indian city (not Bombay). It was about his son and

> family...but I did not confine myself to his experience, relatives, etc. (*Don't Call it Suicide:* VIII).

It's a short play with an 'unusual' title. The plot of the play is based a dilemma—whether to call an unnatural death of a young man (which was neither an accident nor homicide), suicide or not. Mr Nanda, the deceased's father refuses to call the death of the son, a suicide. The protagonist of the play is not Mr Nanda but the dead son.

The play opens with the discussion between Nanda and Sathe on some business matters but soon it takes an inward turn when Mr Nanda chooses to tell Sathe about the tragedy that has befallen on his family. The characters in the play could be divided into two groups: the sentimentalists and the pragmatists. Only Mr Nanda belongs to the first group and the rest belongs to the second.

As persons Mr Nanda and Mrs Nanda can be taken as contrasts. The husband is a conscientious rather a sentimental person who is unable to reconcile to the unnatural death of his 25-year-old son 14 years ago. He broods over the death of his son and breaks down when he recalls the sad incident to his mind. In the first scene, in course of his discussion with Sathe, Nanda says:

> My eldest son...at the age of 25...committed suicide.
>
> (Don't Call it Suicide: I: I: 4)

He adds in the same breath that it is difficult to forget that tragedy. Emotion takes hold of him, and he recalls the sad incident with nostalgia.

> It was about 14 years ago. My eldest son never did well in his exams. He never failed but he did not do well either. He was intelligent and very sensitive, yet somehow, he did not care at all about his school and college, we did not know why. He just wasn't happy there. He complained bitterly all the time. He did not like most of the teachers, and he didn't like most of the students, though he had two or three good friends (Act I, Scene I: 14).

The above lines suggest that the eldest son was unhappy about the ways of the world. Though he was married for 2 years, and his wife was not unhappy with him, he remained calm and silent. Nobody knew what he was up to. Getting a chance (when he was alone in the house), he hanged himself to death. His wife is given shelter by her in-laws. But she is made to work hard in the house. Mr Nanda is sympathetic to her and wants her to be treated more kindly by his wife. Mr Nanda never gets over the incident of his son's death and, therefore, has a soft corner for his daughter-in-law, Meeta. Mrs Nanda, on the other hand, is a pragmatic person who accepts life as it comes. She tells her husband to forget the past and accept life as it comes. She urges upon him to come to terms with life:

> Come on, we have to live a normal life, after all, whatever may have happened in the past. We have to think of our children and grandchildren. Life includes suffering but it is not all suffering.... Whatever happens, I will always do my duty. I am satisfied with my life as it is. Thank God for it (Act I, Scene 1:7).

Contrary to this Mr Nanda is not satisfied with his life. He counters her argument saying:

> I am not satisfied to be what I am. I am not satisfied with my life as it is (Act I, Scene 1:7).

There is a major difference between the husband and the wife in their attitude to Meeta. Ezekiel brings out in a subtle way the intricate relationship between the mother-in-law and the daughter-in-law through the characters of Mrs Nanda and Meeta. When Mr Nanda wants Meeta to meet other members of the family over dinner, Mrs Nanda puts her foot down and asks her not to come out of kitchen. When Mr Nanda proposed to have a family gathering and wants Meeta to meet Sheila and Hari, Mrs Nanda frowns upon him saying that there would be no time for her to do so. She asks Meeta to cook the food and clean the utensils and above all, she is to eat in the kitchen. When Mr Nanda insists on saying that, why can't she eat with us and talk with us? Mrs Nanda retorts: "Alright baba, have your way. I will do the cooking and I will do the serving, and I will do the washing up. Let Meeta eat with you and talk with you." This shows how unkind is Mrs. Nanda to Meeta. Not only that a little later in the play she says, "I allowed my eldest son's widow, Meeta to live with us, but that is only because she is helpful to me in the house."

Hari, Mr Nanda's second son is pragmatic and dominating like his mother. He ill-treats his wife, beats her and always tries to boss over others. He takes his brother to be a sentimental fool and has no sympathy with her sister-in-law. In what looks like a soliloquy Hari tells us about his opinion on his deceased elder brother.

> Why should any student be miserable because some teachers are bad or some students don't care about education? So what? Let them be what they are. Why should we be so sad about it that we actually want to die? Yes, you won't believe it, but my elder brother was like that, 'I feel like killing myself, he would say, as if someone had personally done him great wrong. That's foolish, isn't it? I mean, after all, we have got to survive, haven't we?.... I guess he just wasn't emotionally equipped to cope with life. He was a sensitive idealist. He wasn't— what's the word?—pragmatic' (Act I, Sc. III:13).

It's really shocking that not only Mrs Nanda is rude to Meeta, but all of them Hari and his wife, Malati, Sheila, and her husband, Gopla all ignore her. The only exception being Mr Nanda who has a humanistic approach to life. All these people (son, daughter-in-law, daughter and son-in-law) are self-centred and pragmatic in their approach to life.

Ezekiel makes a dig at certain conventions of the contemporary society through some of the characters. Dominating and beating the wife is prevalent in certain sections of the society. Innocent wives like Malati suffer at the hands of husbands like Hari. Malati states the condition of millions of women in a matter of fact tone:

> The choice for all of, those millions of women in our country whom you mentioned, is between being a happy slave or an unhappy slave. There is no other choice (Act I: IV: 19).

The inhumanity of higher ups in the society comes in for criticism through a conversion between Mr Nanda and Gopal. When Mr Nanda asks Gopal to explain what the latter means by "the inhumanity we see in ordinary, everyday life," Gopal answers:

> Like humiliating people, bossing over them, treating them badly because we are in a position to (Act. I: III: 15).

A little later in the play Gopal becomes explicit in saying that in our country officers misbehave and look down upon the subordinates. Gopal explains:

> A branch manager will always treat another branch manager politely, but he will not be polite to his executive assistants those who work under him, and of course, never to his head clerk or other subordinates (Act I: V: 22).

The play moves to its end by explaining the doubts raised by Mr Nanda in the beginning of the play regarding the cause of his son's suicide. Sathe seems to have the authorial voice when he says:

> It seems to me that some people are entirely different from the rest of us. I'm not thinking of exceptional people, like philosophers, poets and artists. I mean ordinary people. That sounds odd, I know. We treat them in the same way. We take it for granted that they accept all those unpleasant and puzzling things in life which others accept, whether they are ordinary or extraordinary. The particular type I'm talking about is in a class by itself. They have the same good qualities and bad qualities as others have, but there is something else at the source, some essential power that causes non-adjustment to things as they are. It makes many persons in this group feel hopeless, and also sensitive to their own helplessness. Now, surprisingly, I've come to the conclusion that we, the rest of us, have something to learn from them (Act II: II: 29-30).

The failure on the part of a person makes him feel diffident. The attitude of the society towards people who have failed in life, is to say the least, deplorable. Hence, people like Mr Nanda's eldest son who is touchy and sentimental, think to be odd men out and commit suicide. Lack of sympathy on the part of people and inability on their own part to come to terms with life, forces and sentimentalists or persons given to repugnance, as Ezekiel would have us say, to commit suicide.

Mr Sathe's explanation convinced Mr Nanda that he cannot absolve the blame for his son's death. He takes pills and puts an end to his life. Thus, the play which begins against the backdrop of the elder son's suicide ends with the father's suicide. Tragedy is being recreated again in the character of Mr Nanda. This brings to our mind, Ezekiel's observation: "My view is that Indian Society, as a whole is implicated in that and similar situations. The individual way of life, independent, wholly unconventional, has no place among the fixed traditional options."

Mrs Nanda now breaks down and her pragmatism gives way to fatalism. She bursts out:

> I lost a son. Now I've lost my husband. What have I done to deserve this?" (Act II: III: 33).

At that moment Meeta comes to her and comforts her. She could not help saying, 'Oh! my daughter.' The end reminds us of Shakespeare's play, 'Pericles' and T.S. Eliot's closing words of 'Mariana.' Like a drowning person catching at a straw, Mrs Nanda turns to Meeta for support. Hence, the address 'Oh! my daughter!'

> *Don't Call it Suicide* can be read as a criticism of the contemporary society which looks down upon the failed persons and discriminates against the weak. It exposes the ills of the society like unfair treatment given to women in general and widows in particular in our time. Though the ending of the play is ironic, the implicit message is unmistakable.

Mahesh Dattani is the first Indian English Playwright to win the Sahitya Akademi Award for his play, *Final Solutions and Other Plays* for the year 1998. "[Dattani's Work] probes tangled attitudes in contemporary India towards communal differences, consumerism and gender...a brilliant contribution to Indian Drama in English," says Sahitya Akademi award citation. Dattani is a theatre personality. He has experience in the art of production and staging of the plays in various places. Therefore, he has learnt from his experiences, and is quite hopeful about the future reception of his plays. In his *Preface* to *Collected Plays,* Dattani says:

> I am certain that my plays are a true reflection of my time, place and socio-economic background. I am

> hugely excited and curious to know what the future holds for me and my art in the new millennium in a country that has a myriad challenges to face politically, socially, artistically and culturally (2000: XV).

Collected Plays contains eight plays: "Seven Steps Around the Fire," "On a Muggy Night in Mumbai," "Do the Needful," "Final Solutions," "Bravely Fought the Queen," "Tara," "Dance Like a Man" and "Where There's a Will" performed at various places. Dattani's plays are about contemporary reality that one encounters in the metropolis of our country.

He writes about *hijras*, homosexuality and politics in present-day society with confidence and fortitude. The unconventional theme in his plays makes him unacceptable to the conservative audience. But he overcomes these by his forceful dialogue and insight into human nature. In "Seven Steps Around the Fire," he presents the life story of a *hijra* named Kamala, a beautiful eunuch whose murder remained mysterious. The play narrates the plight of the *hijra* community who are equidistant from men and women. They sing and dance at weddings and childbirths. But the irony is that they can neither marry nor give birth to children. Dattani is bold enough to depict the life of the *hijras* who are looked down upon in the society.

Homosexuality as a theme has been dealt with two of Dattani's plays namely *Bravely Fought the Queen* and *A Muggy Night in Mumbai.* M.K. Naik draws our attention to the employment of the theme of homosexuality in the following words:

> The motif of homosexuality which is touched upon in *Bravely Fought the Queen* is at the centre of *A Muggy Night in Mumbai.* The play presents a group of well-to-do homosexuals in Bombay, their changing mutual relationship, their revelations, their self-delusions and self-discoveries. Though they are all sailing in the same boat, each has his/her own oar to put in, his/her own flag to hoist. Kamalesh is weak and sensitive: Sharad is his exact opposite, with his jaunty nonchalance. Ed assumes a double identity, with Prakash as his second *avatar.* Bunny is true to the 'kindred point' of home and the Homo Den; he is a good husband at home and a very competent one in his bedroom, while he enjoys

> himself as a gay soul in the company of the initiated. Ranjit solves his problem by going abroad where he feels he will be more readily accepted; and Deepali is a militant lesbian, who declares, 'Every time I menstruate, I thank God I am a woman.' Totally free of guilt, she is strong and bold enough to strike Ed when he becomes violent. The wedding music heard constantly in the background in the final Act is an ironic commentary on the lives of these homosexuals for whom 'marriage can only be a doubly dirty twice-four letter word' (*Littcrit* June-Dec. 2001:51).

It seems that Mahesh Dattani feels that homosexuality is a subject that people want to discuss but do not talk about because of social taboos. Hence, he uses it as a theme in his plays to give a chance to the people to look into the problem intently.

Final Solutions, a play in three Acts, deals with a political theme. It is replete with communal tensions that bedevil our society. I concur with M.K. Naik when he makes an explication of the theme of the play in the following words:

> *Final Solutions* is the only political play written by Dattani so far. Two Muslim boys, Javed and Babban, take shelter in the house of Ramnik Gandhi, a Hindu businessman, while communal riot rages outside. During the course of their interaction, Ramnik reveals the past and confesses how his father and grandfather had burnt down the shop of a rival, Muslim businessman, in a communal riot forty years ago. Ramnik's mother also remembers the travails of Partition, and how both Hindus and Muslims suffered then. Babban's comment at the end is significant: 'if we understand and believe in one another, nothing can be destroyed.' But Dattani doesn't end the play on this romantic note. The Chorus, which has the last word, adds, 'One reality cannot accept/another reality.'
>
> "Allied to this is another recurrent theme in Dattani: familial relationships. Ramnik never ceases to hear the harsh rattling of the skeleton in the family cupboard, which has given him an outsize guilt complex Hardika carries her hatred of her in-laws, who persecuted her in the best traditions of the Hindu joint family, as a

> perpetual chip on her wrinkled shoulders; and Smita, the daughter of Ramnik knows that her secret love for Babban is a hopeless passion" (*Ibidem* 51-52).

Dattani's plays holds mirror unto contemporary Indian society in certain respects. The struggle for individual human beings for a space in the society is uppermost in his mind and therefore, he makes an attempt in his plays to create this "space" for them. In course of an article titled, "Hard at Play" Samita Bhatia makes a pertinent comment on Dattani's plays.

> There is also a common thread that binds Dattani's plays. He explains, "Thematically, I talk about the areas where the individual feels excluded. My plays are about such people who are striving to expand this space."

His characters—whether in *Where There's a Will, Dance Like a Man, Tara, On a Muggy Night in Mumbai, Seven Steps Around Fire*—boldly fight for this space and "perhaps acceptance." But Dattani corrects himself: "They live on the fringes of society and are not looking for acceptance, but are struggling to grab as much fringe-space for themselves as they can. Thus, Dattani's plays take up what have been described as 'invisible issues' of Indian society, combining verbal ingenuity with a strong visual element" (*Graphiti* 2 April 2000:7).

Apart from these three noted Playwrights, some minor Indian English playwrights have also published their plays in the last two decades of the twentieth century.

Vera Sharma's *Life is Like That* (1997), Derek Antao's *Give Us This Day Our Black Sheet* (1980), Gieve Patel's *Mister Behram* (1988), Dina Mehta's *Brides Are Not for Burning* (1993) and Manjula Padmanabhan's *Harvest* (1998) are some of the well-known plays in Indian English Literature. M.K. Naik makes an observation on recent Indian English drama with special reference to the plays of Manjula Padmanabhan, Dina Mehta and Poile Sengupta in the following words:

> Manjula Padmanabhan created history when her play *Harvest* (1998) won the first prize in the first Onassis International Cultural Competition. This is the first time that an Indian English dramatist has won an honour abroad. *Harvest* is a tautly constructed futuristic play,

> a frightening vision of a cannibalistic future, in which the sale of human organs has become all too common. The time of this dystopia is the year 2010, and the setting, Bombay. "Interplanta Services" arrange for the sale and transplant of organs of willing Indians into the jaded bodies of rich Americans. The play shows how a transaction of this kind affects the family of our on the one hand, and two Americans—Ginni and Virgil on the other.
>
> Padmanabhan's recent play *Lights Out* has appeared in *Body Blows: Women, Violence and Survival: Three Plays* (2000), which also contains Dina Mehta's *Getting Away with Murder* and Poile Sengupta's *Mangalam.* As the title of the collection indicates, the leitmotif of all the three plays is the victimization of women in Indian Society. *Lights Out* presents the tragic spectacle of the daily rape of women, watched at a distance by the middle-class characters. Leela and Naina are anguished by the cries for help, but the men, Bhaskar and Mohan quieten their conscience by arguing that the victims are after all only prostitutes, not "decent" women. In *Mangalam,* Sengupta shows the members of a middle-class Tamil Brahmin joint family commenting on a play about the victim of a rape but ironically enough, the viewers themselves are involved in domestic violence. The use of the "play within a play" technique enhances the ironic effect. (2002:213).

Following Mahesh Dattani, R. Raj Rao has written interesting One-Act Plays titled *The Wisest Fool on Earth and Other Plays* (1996) on the theme of homosexuality. And G. Prasanti has published a play titled *The Myth Resurrected* (1991) in which an attempt has been made to interpret the Oedipus myth from Indian point of view.

Indian English drama has not developed the way Indian English poetry or fiction grew because of the lack of opportunities to stage it. Moreover, English is not the language spoken by the common people in the street. Lack of contact with the spoken word has crippled the dramatists to write plays in English. But nonetheless, we have some good plays in English.

Works Cited

Bhatia, Bhatia. "Hard at Play." *Graphiti (The Telegraph* Magazine 2 April 2002).

Dattani, Mahesh. *Collected Plays.* New Delhi: Penguin Books, 2000.

Ezekiel, Nissim. *Don't Call it Suicide.* Madras: MacMillan, 1993.

Karnad, Girish. *The Fire and the Rain.* New Delhi: Oxford University Press, 1998.

Maya, D. "Karnad's The Fire and the Rain: A Return to Indigenous Tradition." *The Literary Criterion* 36:4 (2001).

Murthy, Anantha, Prasana, Girish, Karnad. "Girish Karnad, the Play wright: A Discussion." *Indian Literature* 169. Sept.-Oct. 1995.

Naik, M.K. "Cinderella Still: Recent Indian English Drama." *Litterit 27:* 1-2, (June-Dec. 2001).

Naik, M.K. and Shyamala A. Narayan. *Indian English Literature* 1980-2000: *A Critical Survey.* New Delhi: Pencraft International, 2001.

6
Postmodern Indian English Autobiography

The first generation of Indian English Autobiographers belongs to the Independence era. Many of our top leaders and freedom fighters like Gandhi, Nehru, Maulana Abul Kalam Azad wrote their autobiographies during that period. In fact, Nehru's *An Autobiography* is the best book in that genre in our country. In the Post-Independence era Nirad C. Chaudhuri published his autobiography titled, *The Autobiography of an Unknown Indian* in 1952 and earned a name as a writer both at home and abroad. Dom Moraes wrote his autobiography at an early age titled, *My Son's Father* in 1965. Apart from these well-known writers quite a few other writers also wrote their autobiographies before and after Independence. Such books are outside the purview of my book. In this chapter an attempt has been made to make an assessment of autobiographies written in the postmodern period.

Important books of autobiography in the postmodern period include R.K. Narayan's *My Days* (1986), Nirad C. Chaudhuri's *Thy Hand, Great Anarch* (1987), Kamala Das' *My Story* (1988), Dom Moraes' *Never at Home* (1992) and a few other books written by academics and scientists. Before analysing these books let me make an observation on the literary qualities of Indian English autobiography in general.

Autobiography as a genre of literature is a metaphor of the self and it's a journey on the part of the autobiographer from the known to the unknown. It can be taken as an attempt to find an objective correlative for the self. James Olney describes autobiography as, 'a monument of the self as it is becoming, a metaphor of the self at the summary moment of composition' and further states that its objective is to build, "a metaphoric bridge from subjective sub-consciousness to objective reality" (1992:36).

I concur with Ranjana Harish's elucidation of the points made in James Olney's book given in the following passage:

> In the same book Olney discusses several male-authored self-narratives to illustrate how each one of them invents a unique, exclusive and fresh metaphor to express the self. Jung, Montaigne, Mill, Newman, Darwin or Gandhi— each of these men invents a special objective correlative to reach his reader. Upto this point Olney's theorizing is fine. However, as he proceeds, his theorizing acquires a patriarchal tone. In an imperative tone he prescribes preconditions for the metaphorizing viewpoint and says that such a viewpoint "must be" (1) unitary, (2) specially human and (3) personally unique. This part of his theory excludes the minorities from the metaphorizing process. Like his master Georges Gusdorf, who advanced the "individualistic paradigm of centrally located isolate autobiographical self" (Gusdorf 29) and thus kept out the marginals like blacks and women from the purview of autobiographical writings/studies, Olney too overlooks the marginal identity here. He thus confirms his affinity with the school of critical thinking which looked upon minorities either as misfit to be autobiographical subjects because of their lack of isolate individual self or maintained silence over their attempts at autobiography writing and thus shut them cut of the canonical discourse. But these patriarchal theorists, says Susan Stanford Friedman, missed a very important point, namely, "self-creation and self- consciousness are profoundly different for women, minorities and non-Westerners" (Private Self 35). She further argues that Gusdorf s theory does not take into consideration the importance of the culturally imposed group identity for the minorities, including women. If "separate selfhood is the very motive of creation" [autobiography] and if autobiography is "a mirror in which the 'individual reflects his own image" (Gusdorf 33) then this mirror does not reflect

> back a unique image to woman. "It projects an image of WOMAN, a category that is supposed to define the living woman's identity" says Shari Benstock. As a result "an awareness of the meaning of the cultural category 'woman' [dictates] the patterns of woman's individual destiny" (Private Self 31, 41). The post-80s feminist theorists like Estelle Jelinek, Shari Benstock, Sheila Rowbotham, Nancy Chodorow, Susan Friedman, Maison and others expose the inapplicability of Gusdorfian theory to the autobiographies by the minorities and assert the need for a separate poetics for the autobiographies by the minorities which will take into consideration the socio-cultural attributes of their personality (JDE 26:2, 1998-99:39-40).

It is said that "autobiography is the mirror in which the individual reflects his own image." But if one falls in love with one's own image, he is likely to magnify it and hence, in the process will get distorted. Some critics have tended to divide male and female autobiographers into two categories because of gender consciousness. I would like to return to Ranjana Harish on the question of making a diachronic study of autobiography, as observed in the following paragraphs:

> Following Georges Gusdorf theorists of autobiography from Ronald Barthes to James Olney have persisted in maintaining the idea of centrally located isolate I as the precondition for autobiography. "Separate selfhood is the very motive of (autobiographical) creation" asserted James Olney (1978: 22). Under the influence of these critics there developed a school of critical thinking which valued autobiography as a genre of individualistic self. Naturally this school believed that a culture which did not encourage individualistic image of self would not provide proper soil to autobiography. Their master Gusdorf had gone up to the extent of saying that in ancient civilization of the East the genre could not flourish at all due to the rejection of ego by those civilizations on metaphysical plane and whatever scattered autobiographical work was done in those countries was dismissed by him as nothing but "cultural transplant." The metaphysical stand of

> Gusdorf reminds one of great Sanskrit scholars like Keith and Winternitz who in their memorable studies of classical Sanskrit drama used metaphysical ground of Brahminic world view to explain the absence of tragedy in the classical literature.

Lately, since 70's feminist theorists like Patricia Meyer Spacks, Estelle Jelinek, Shari Banstock, Nancy Chodorow, Sheila Rowbotham, Nancy Friedman and others have started questioning the traditional paradigm of isolate self on the ground that it doesn't take into consideration minority classes as, to quote Friedman, "self, self-creation and self-consciousness are profoundly different for women, minorities and many non-Western peoples." In these critics' view Gusdorflan theory of centrally located isolate selfhood leads to misreading and marginalizations of autobiographical texts by minorities. Thus, to their mind, the critical tradition of the genre supports restrictive and unspoken cannon of White Male autobiographers. These male critics have no doubt advanced the understanding of autobiography greatly but their insistence on individualistic paradigms for the self-have, once again to quote Friedman, "obscured the presence and significance of women's autobiography in literary tradition" (*The Literary Criterion* 31: 1-2, 1996:27-29).

No doubt, there is bound to be difference in perception between autobiographers belonging to different cultures. Similarly, there could be a difference between men and women as autobiographers because of gender inhibitions. But to say that women will shy away from describing love and sex in their autobiographies is to tell half-truths. If men glorify their own success or individual selves, women also do so or at least capable of doing so. An autobiography is not merely the life history of an individual, but it is also a reflection of its times. The autobiographies of M.K. Gandhi, Jawaharlal Nehru and Nirad C. Chaudhuri are cases in point. It is most incorrect reprehensible to divide autobiographies and autobiographers on the basis of gendre. Post-modern women are not prudes in public. Kamala Das' autobiography, *My Story* bears testimony to it.

Before making an analysis of Indian English autobiography in the post-1980 era, I would like to dispel the doubts expressed by Georges Gasdorf (as quoted by Ranjana Harish) about the ability of Indians to write autobiographies:

> The Wisdom of India considers personality an evil illusion and sees salvation in depersonalization which renders Indians unfit as autobiographical selves (*Ibidem* 32).

This is far- from truth. Nehru's *An Autobiography,* Maulana Azad's *Indian Wins Freedom* and M.C. Chagla's *Roses in December,* Gandhi's *My Experiments with Truth* and Nirad C. Chaudhuri's *The Autobiography of an Unknown Indian* to state only a few titles are enough to give a lie to Gasdorf's statement.

R.K. Narayan's *My Days* is a significant autobiography by the foremost Indian English novelist. In this memoir Narayan tells the story of his life in Mysore. The publisher's note to the book provides a clue to the subject.

> The story begins in a grandmother's garden in Madras, with pets who come to no good end—monkeys and peacocks and enraged cats. There is school, bizarrely inconvenient to a boy with his mind on other, better ways of spending time—like training grasshoppers, scouting, football, and generally becoming part of the excitement of life around him. In Mysore later, difficulties arise when the schoolmaster father (a man of commanding personality) and the dreaming son do not see eye to eye on the need to pass exams. Comical interludes abound, but the name of Narayan gradually takes on weight in Important Circles, and there are unpredictable negotiations with English publisher (1986).

Though *My Days* was written in 1974-75, it was issued in Orient paperback imprint in 1986. As Meena Sodhi has rightly pointed out that, "Narayan's personal life in *My Days* reads like any of his novels, with his emphasis on the Indian domestic scene, the middle class, especially the small segment of agricultural community, and the personal relationships. The Indian middle class, which Narayan says, is the only class he understands, is beautifully represented not only in his autobiography, but also in *Swami and Friends* and *The English Teacher*—the two novels which have drawn heavily from the facts of Narayan's life" (1999: 25).

R.K. Narayan describes the making of the film *The Guide* out of his novel of the same title with some detail in chapter fifteen of the book, *My Days.* From Devanand's approach to Lord Mountbatten assurance to persuade Queen Elizabeth to attend the world premiere of *The Guide* in London, everything has been recorded here.

Dom Moraes gives an interesting account of a phone call made by a friend which prompted him to choose the title *Never At Home* as a sequel to his autobiography, *My Son's Father.* Moraes had cut off the phone line, (metaphorically speaking) by instructing his household not to receive a phone call during that part of the day when he was busy with writing the second part of his autobiography. As he finished writing the autobiography, he had the following phone call from a friend:

> "Where in hell have you been?" he asked. "I have been phoning you all day for a week. I've even phoned you at night, and they say you're somewhere else, they don't know where. Are you never at home?" (Moraes 1992:341).

Never At Home deals with less than two decades *(i.e.,* from 1974 to 1990) of Moraes' life but that is the period of anguish for him when he searched for an identity being alienated from his mad mother, his first wife and his motherland. Meena Sodhi makes an interesting comment on this book in the following words:

> *Never At Home* picks up from where *My Son's Father* left off. It moves at a fervent speed and as we accompany Moraes on his journey across the globe we see the world through his eyes; we meet dozens of leaders and statesmen. As a writer he covered events like the Eichmann trial in Israel; travelled in Asia, Africa, the America; made television documentaries for the BBC, wrote for a number of foreign newspapers and worked for the U.N. As an investigative journalist, he rushed around the world in pursuit of stories, like perhaps no other Indian journalist has ever done. Therefore, it is not merely a case of name-dropping which is seen in the book, Moraes has done serious reporting too. "A poet, a restless pilgrim, and a keen observer of the world around, Dom Moraes is remarkable as a writer

> and a commentator on man's struggle for survival. His life-story is both fascinating and poignant. This account is filled up with numerous incidents and anecdotes which are described distinctly. The book has good prose by an Indian writer, even though Moraes frequently stresses that he does not want to be merely a prose writer" (*Critical Practice* 4:2, 1997:34).

The search for identity always haunted him. The poet in him all the time helped him to assume a kind of identity in spite of his personal difficulties in life. Thus, Moraes writes:

> Everyone wears some kind of mask, which is expressed in the face he or she presents to the world. A mask of this kind is not difficult to invent. For example, my mask was that of a rather casual person, unperturbed by what was happening around me, known as a poet, experienced in the world, a veteran war correspondent. I could respond to the demands of my mask, and offer its smile, with some confidence, to others. Behind this mask, I thought, lay my identity, which was not to be exposed. It was by keeping the identity, not the mask, that I remained alive. The identity contained all the experiences the mask had but experienced them differently. A great part of my identity lay in my ability to write poetry, and also in knowing exactly what world I belonged to (Moraes 1992:310).

As the search for 'belongingness' continues, Moraes could not help saying, "I am waiting to be at home, where I don't know yet." The book ends with an interesting account of his meeting with the great Kannad a writer, Karanth.

> Sometime in 1976 (it must have been June or July, since it was raining heavily in the southern state of Karnataka), I went to meet a famous local writer called Karanth. He was small, with a white moustache, and very old, but exceptionally lively for his years. In the front-room of his house, he awaited me with tea, sweetmeats of many sorts, including Mars bars, and a chalkboard on which various numbers and mathematical equations had been scrawled. "It is surprising for you that I wanted to meet you," he said, "is it not? But apart from being a great writer, I am a

> student of numerology." He pointed to the board, and intoned four words once familiar on British television, "This is your life."
>
> I expected everyone I had ever known to emerge one by one from the wings: that is, from the kitchen that opened off the room we were in. Nobody did. "Look at the board," said Dr Karanth. "You were born on the 19th of July 1938. Do you understand what that means? Nineteen, think hard of that number. It is the number with which your whole life is involved. Think of the year 1938. That is a number divisible by nineteen, is it not?" Outside, a small rain was falling, scented by the flowers on which it fell.
>
> This deflected my attention from him for a moment. But, schoolmaster-like, he produced a cane, with the tip of which he rapped the chalkboard. "In 1957," he said, "you won the Hawthornden prize in Britain. Now tell me, what is 1957 divisible by? By nineteen. And, at that time, you were nineteen years old. Is that not proof enough of your affinity with this number? It is. It is. My good boy, I tell you, it is proof!"
>
> I had made some mathematical calculations, and said, 'Dr Karanth, this is 1976, which is also divisible by nineteen. Nothing very remarkable has happened to me this year.' He replied, "Oh, my dear, my darling boy, but it has. You have met me."
>
> Outside, amidst the many pleasant smells of his garden I reflected that for the next piece of luck in my life I would have to wait until 1995. "I am waiting" (*Ibidem* 341-2).

Dr Karanth proved to be right. In 1995, Moraes was conferred with Sahitya Akademi Award for his book of verse, *Serendip* for the year 1994. At last, Moraes must have felt 'at home' in his motherland.

A group of women autobiographers have published their life stories in the last two decades of the twentieth century. Ranjana Harish gives a list of such writers in the following words:

> Complete rejection of needle as a metaphor of self is a striking feature of the autobiographers writing during the last two decades. It's, in a way, indicative

of the socio-economic and politico-cultural change in the status of woman in Indian society. The changing socio-economic structure of Indian society, along with women's own increased self-awareness regarding self-worth, brings change in gender-roles too. From the object-position now women assume subject-position. Autobiographers like Vijaya Raje Scindia (1985), Kamala Devi Chattopadhyay (1986), Edila Gaitonde (1987), Tara Ali Baig (1988), Prema Naidu (1990), Indira Goswami (1990), Sharanjeet Shan (1991), Savitri Bajaj (1991), Raj Thapar (1991), Mina Alexander (1992) and Vimla Patil (1996) record Indian women's faith in the pen as the metaphor of their collective as well as individual selves. They look upon education and employment as the only means to create a rightful female space in the society. Three very striking features of the autobiographies of these decades are: (1) Women's increasing awareness of their collective identity as the greatest source of strength and hence their involvement in creating sisterhood. (2) Their complete rejection of feminine culture broadly covered under the metaphor of the needle in the earlier autobiographies. (3) Their unflinching faith in the pen—the signifier of authority, respectability and male sphere (JDE 26:2, 1988-89:45).

Kamala Das' autobiography My *Story* created sensations in our country. It was reissued in 1988 after first being published in 1976. Her frank description of love and sex created controversy in India. But the language in her hand becomes a lively form of expression. That is the redeeming feature of her autobiography. Primarily being a poet, she is conscious of her choice of themes in her poetry.

Though autobiographies have been written and read long ago, their study as a genre is recent and uncritical in India and even in Britain. Roypascal's *Design and Truth in Autobiography* published in 1960 is said to be the first serious book on autobiography, an improvement over H.N. Wethered's work, *The Curious Art of Autobiography* published in 1956. Peter Abbs traces the origin of the first use of the world, "autobiography" to the following sources:

It is pertinent to note that the word 'autobiography' was first employed in 1809—at the height of the Romantic period—and that the first formal use of the word 'autobiography' in publishing was in 1834 when W.P. Scargill's volume *The Autobiography* of a Dissenting Minister was printed. But the form of autobiography goes back through fourteen centuries to St Augustine's *Confessions* written in the second half of the fourth century. The words 'autobiography' and 'confessions'— and the particular historical tides on which they bob—are charged with meanings which we must not overlook. The confessions of the Christian period can be viewed from one perspective as the sacrament of confession metamorphosed into literary form; the Autobiographies of the Romantic and Modern periods can thus be understood as those confessions secularized. ...confessions, in their traditional form crave forgiveness, autobiography desires understanding. Confessions are devoted to salvation, autobiographies to individuation *(The New Pelican Guide to English Literature: 8. The Present* (1987:513).

The title of the second part of Nirad C. Chaudhuri's book, *Thy Hand, Great Anarch*! (India: 1921-1952) is taken from Alexander Pope's following quotation:

> Lo! thy dreed Empire, 'Chaos! is restor'd;
> Light dies before thy uncreating word;
> Thy hand, great Anarch! let's the curtain fall;
> And Universal Darkness buries All.

In his introduction to the book, Chaudhuri makes his intention as well as the scope of his autobiography clear when he asserts that, "this book continues the story of my life and thoughts from the point of time at which it was left in *The Autobiography of an Unknown Indian* published in 1951." This book is not complete in the sense that it has not covered the last part of the author's life. Chaudhuri is aware of this limitation of the book and admits it too.

> However, even now I have not been able to give the book the end one would expect it to have. Of course, autobiographies cannot have the same logical end as biographies always have. But they are generally brought down to the time when they are written. This book falls short of even that by thirty-two years, for it only covers

> my 'working life,' which began in 1921 and came to a close at the end of 1952 (1987: XIII).

Thy Hand Great Anarch runs into nine hundred sixty-four pages (Introduction and Index excluded) and is divided into ten books covering the period between 1921 and 1952. It is an amalgam of Chaudhuri's life and Indian history during that period. The "Epilogue" is the climax of the book which shows the metamorphosis of Chaudhuri, the non-believer into a believer. This is a very significant development in the book. Chaudhuri writes:

> 'I believe in order to understand.' In the light of my early mental development, this would appear to be the strangest confession for me to make at the end of my life (*Ibidem* 940).

The decadence of the modern period, particularly in the second half of the twentieth century, springs from intellectual failure to contain it. Arid what pains Chaudhuri most is the lack of faith among the people. Thus, he regrets to say that, "the problem of sustaining faith would not have been so difficult had there been a frank recognition by the thinkers of our age of the reality of the decadence in social life and mores" (*Ibidem* 961). However, Chaudhuri does not lose faith in human possibility and ends the book with a fervent plea to take note of duality in human condition. Thus, he writes:

> "...the human situation in its fundamental character is not worse than what it always has been, only the scale of the conflict between progress and decadence is infinitely larger. Men of faith, believing in a higher dispensation in the universe than man's will, have always been bewildered by the duality in their existence" (*Ibidem* 963).

Two interesting autobiographies by two distinguished Professors of English—that is, C.D. Narasimhaiah's *N for Nobody. The Autobiography of an English Teacher* (1991) and P.S. Sundaram's *Simple Simon* (1998)—provide an insight into English studies in India in the period just preceding and following Independence. M.K. Naik and Shyamala A. Narayan have made a perceptive comment on these two books in the following words:

> Narasimhaiah's *N for Nobody: The Autobiography of an English Teacher* (1991) reveals a lot about the growth of English in Indian universities in the last four decades. Narasimhaiah's literary criticism is usually couched in a no-nonsense style, closely linked to the speaking voice demonstrating the finer points of a work of literature. *N for Nobody* shows that he is capable of a variety of literary styles. The second chapter, on Mysore, is lyrical in its intensity, while the tension of emotion held in check is almost palpable in the last chapter describing the death of his younger son Sanjay in an appendicitis operation. The tone is generally frank and dispassionate, with a willingness to laugh at himself and others.
>
> P.S. Sundaram, teacher, poet, critic, and translator from Tamil and Sanskrit, calls his autobiography *Simple Simon* (1998). It was published after his death in June 1998, and shows that the straightforward Sundaram lacked the wiles to rise high in the hierarchy (being a Brahmin may also have been a handicap as government policy is committed to the uplift of the backward castes). The autobiography reveals that merit is not the only criterion for career advancement in Indian universities (2001: 222-23).

C.D. Narasimhaiah's love for English language and England, prompts Bidhubhusan Das to compare his autobiography with that of Nirad C. Chaudhuri's *The Autobiography of an Unknown India*. Das observes:

> It is here that one remembers another eminent Indian, Nirad Chaudhuri, who migrated to Oxford to settle down there for this reason. The resemblance of this book to *The Autobiography of an Unknown Indian,* cannot be missed. All of which points to one singular aspect of the minds of both authors, their adumbration of intellectual aristocracy which still receives recognition in England, not in our country generally speaking, although that has been prominently our cultural tradition (*Indian Literature* No. 149, 1992:168).

Some of our writers, scientists, diplomats and cartoonists have published their autobiographies in the post-1980 period. They include Rushin Bond's *Scenes from a Writer's Life: A Memoir* (1997), R.K. Laman's *The Tunnel of Time* (1998),

P. Lal's *Lessons* (1991), Karan Singh's *Heir Apparent: An Autobiography* (1982) and *Autobiography 1931-1967* (1989), T.N. Kaul's *Ambassadors Need Not Lie* (1988, 89 in three volumes), K.P.S. Menon's *One Thousand Full Moons* (1987), P.N. Hasker's One More Life (1990), A.P.J. Abdul Kalam's Wings *of Fire: An Autobiography* (1990) and a few other autobiographies. Some of these works are only for historical records without any great literary merit.

Indian English Autobiography is not as developed as Indian English poetry or fiction. It is as neglected as Indian English drama. That is because a good number of autobiographies are lacking in literary style. Nonetheless, the autobiographies of Nirad C. Chaudhuri, Dom Moraes and C.D. Narasimhaiah stand out as good works in that genre in the postmodern period.

Works Cited

Abbs, Peter. "Autobiography: Quest for Identity." *The New Pelican Guide to English Literature: 8. The Present.* Ed. Boris Ford. London: Penguin Books, 1987.

Chaudhuri, Nirad. C. *Thy Hand, Great Anarch!* London: Chatto and Windus Ltd., 1987.

Das, Bidhubhusan. "Insight into Human Life" rev. *N for Nobody: An Autobiography of an English Teacher. Indian Literature 149,* May-June 1992.

Das, Kamala. *My Story.* New Delhi: Sterling Publishers, 1988.

Harish, Ranjana. "Pen and Needle: The Changing Metaphors of Self in Autobiographies by Women in Post-Independence India." *The Journal of the Department of English* 26:2 (1998-99).

——. "In the Cultural Hall of Mirrors: Issue of Gender Genre Incompatibility of Women's Autobiography." *The Literary Criterion* 31:1-2 (1996).

Moraes, Dom. *Never At Home.* New Delhi: Penguin Books, 1992.

Naik, MX and Shyamala A. Narayan. *Indian English Literature 1980-2000: A Critical Survey.* New Delhi: Pencraft International, 2001.

Narayan, R.K. *My Days.* New Delhi: Orient Paperbooks,1986.

Olney, James. *Metaphors of Self: The Meaning of Autobiography.* Princeton: Princeton University Press, 1972.

Sodhi, Meena. "Dom Moraes' *Never at Home: Alienation and Search for Identity" Critical Practice* 4:2 (June 1997).

——. *Indian English Writing. The Autobiographical Mode.* New Delhi: Creative Books, 1999.

7
Conclusion

In the concluding chapter of my book, I would like to make an assessment of the achievement of Indian English Literature in the postmodern period without overlooking its deficiency. At the outset, I would dwell upon the inadequacy of this literature. First, Indian English Literature does not have readers at the grass-roots level. That is, common people of our country do not read it or have access to it. It is a literature of the second language-learner readers. In other words, it is read by the people whose second language, or third language is English. In plain language, English educated readers have access to this body of literature. Except Nagaland in no other state English is the first language in our country. To put it more clearly, I should say that when Oriya literature or Hindi literature for that matter any Bhasa literature is read by common readers in that language, Indian English literature is read only by English educated Indians. So, it is correct to say that Indian English literature is not a mass literature in our country.

Secondly, Postmodern Indian English literature is city-oriented or urban based. It is about middle class, upper-middle class or the elite class. It aims at western recognition and gets respectability at home because of its acceptability abroad. It is our neo-colonial attitude that places Indian English literature above Bhasa literature. For example, we eulogise post-1980 Indian English novelists because they have been honoured abroad and place them above old writers like R.K. Narayan, Mulk Raj Anand, Raja Rao and Arun Joshi. This attitude has been criticised by Alstair Niven in the following words:

> Everyone cottons on the newer generation of writers starting with Rushdie as though they revolutionalise Indian writing. But they have predecessors just as good

> in some cases better. I feel rather sad that R.K. Narayan, Mulk Raj Anand, Raja Rao, Nirad C. Chaudhuri, G.V. Desani and Kamala Markandaya are sidelined today. I think it would be hard to find a more fastidious use of language than in Narayan. Chaudhuri handled the English language magisterially. Anand made an interesting hybrid with Punjabi phrasing and Raja Rao's Sanskrit influences brought in a metaphysical dimension. Don't underestimate the older writers (2000: III).

Thirdly, Indian English literature is not very representative of Indian ethos and sensibility, for it does not portray the common Indian people authentically. Even when Indian English fiction writers try to portray the common mass in their fiction, they put words into their mouth which they have never uttered. What I mean to say is that when a Bhasa writer portrays a character, he uses the language actually used by the character in the real-life situation, and hence, his character appears to be life like. But Indian English writer uses a language or an idiom which the character is supposed to speak in a situation and therefore, it lacks authenticity.

The lacunae, if we may say so, of Indian English literature as stated above, notwithstanding, the achievement of this body of literature in the Postmodern period is immense and therefore, commendable. Indian English literature aroused academic interest and gained acceptability in our universities as a course of study in this period. That is, because it has been able to establish its credential as an Indian literature. For example, Indian English poetry which blossomed in the mid-seventies, got recognition as a substantial body of literature by the National Akademi of Letters. Awards were given in quick succession by the Sahitya Akademi to individual books of poems such as Jayanta Mahapatra's *Relationship* in 1981, Nissim Ezekiel's *Latter-Day Psalms* in 1983, Keki N. Daruwalla's *The Keeper of the Dead* in 1984, Kamala Das' *Collected Poems* Vol. I in 1985 and Shiv K. Kumar's *Trapfalls in the Sky* in 1987. Later on Dom Moraes' *Serendip* and A.K. Ramanujan's *Collected Poems* were given the Sahitya Akademi award in 1994 and 1999 respectively. Postmodern Indian English poetry has an idiom of its own. Indian English poets have successfully recreated contemporary Indian reality in their poetry. A.K. Ramanujan's *Black Hen,* Jayanta Mahapatra's *Shadow Space* and *Bare Face,* Shiv K. Kumar's *Woolgathering* and *Thus Spake the Buddha,* Kamala Das' *Only the Soul knows how to Sing,* Keki N. Daruwalla's *A Summer of Tigers* and Dom Moraes' *Serendip* are some of the best-known books of poems in recent years. Both in themes and in techniques Indian English poetry has established its authenticity that at once distinguishes it from poetry written in English elsewhere in the world. The humanistic touch in Ezekiel's poetry, the re-creation of *The Mahabharata* episode in Shiv K. Kumar's poetry and evocation of rural scene in Jayanta Mahapatra's poetry show how the once colonised 'other' has written back to the 'centre' and the 'periphery' has moved to the centre. Here are a few extracts from some of the important poems:

> May you be
> poet, painter, scholar,
> thinker, musician
> even if you create nothing that matters
> except your life, which too
> has to be created. ('Blessings')

In these lines Ezekiel asserts that life has to be created not lived upon. The truth of the statement is undeniable.

In "Lord Krishna to Arjuna" after having explained the mystery of the Universe to Arjuna, Lord Krishna asks him to light the forces of evil.

Kumar writes:

> The pick up your bow and arrow, O, Warrior,
> and fight to set the crooked straight,
> Your destiny way etched on your palm at birth.

The exhortation of Lord Krishna to Arjuna helps Kumar to understand life. Like T.S. Eliot, Kumar realises in the end the futility of life and pines for '*Shantih*':

> The way inside is the way out
> to understanding—
> that each paradox carries two faces:
> bud and insect, beginning and end.
> And beyond all this
> is pure void, *neti*
> the essence of perennial tranquility
> *Shantih*! ('Meditation')

Postmodern poetry moves from nationalism to transnationalism, when our poets speak not only of our country but of the whole world. The violence that rocks the world is a curse that all the countries are to live with now and it is in this sense New Delhi is no different from Jerusalem and Nicaragua. Thus, writes Jayanta Mahapatra:

> Why wait to be free of history
> when you are now in it?
> secrets will begin to speak
> ashes soak in the rivers.
> And the streets
> go on enjoying their dead—
> either in Jerusalem
> Or in Delhi or distant Nicaragua. ("The Waiting")

The appeal of Indian English poetry is immense. But one thing that disturbs us most is that there is no major new voice in Indian English poetry. The old poets who began their career in the 1960s and 1970s, they still dominate the poetic scene. However, this with not the case with Indian English fiction.

The most significant achievement in Postmodern Indian English Literature is in the field of fiction. The confidence with which our novelists write fiction is commendable. Both thematically and technically they have broken a new ground. Novelists like Amitav Ghosh, Shashi Tharoor, Upamanyu Chatterjee, Vikram Seth, Vikram Chandra and Arundhati Roy have extended the thematic range of Indian English fiction by working on the everyday reality like broken marriages, violence, lawlessness, man-woman relationship in our society and themes like Indian music, national myths in contemporary situations. *The Mahabharata* is the vast reservoir of Indian myths and some of our writers like Shashi Tharoor have worked on the myths embodied in that great epic. The Postmodern novelists have discarded the grand narratives of earlier writers Mulk Raj Anand, R.K. Narayan and Raja Rao, and adopted a form of narrative which has come to be known as 'narratives of disintegration.'

Indian English fiction in the eighties and after is known for its use of language. There is a good deal of code mixing in fiction. Words from Bhasa languages such as 'Kaki,' 'Mami,'

'Jethamoshai,' 'Charpais,' 'Chowkidar,' 'Pan,' 'Ashram,' and a host of others are used freely in Indian English fiction.

The novelists in the Postmodern era have successfully used parody as a mode of narration in Indian English fiction. Portraying characters n terms of myths embodied in our epics serves the purpose of giving recognition to them and gaining public acceptance. Reality of life is shown in terms of struggle between 'dharma' and 'adharma,' and the battle of Kurukshetra is not yet over. In the words of modern Ved Vyas, in *The Great Indian Novel* 'Life is Kurukshetra,' 'history is Kurukshetra.'

Postmodern Indian English novel successfully meets the challenges of Bhasa novels in our country and postcolonial novels abroad by creating a new idiom for creative expression and portraying reality in terms of contemporary society. Love and sex are depicted in Indian English novel with frankness and without any inhibitions. History of recent past becomes the subject matter of some of the novels. Partition of India is a much-used theme in post-1980 fiction.

Indian English short story has developed considerably in the last two decades of the twentieth century. Ruskin Bond, Manoj Das, and the great trio, Mulk Raj Anand, Raja Rao, R.K. Narayan have enriched this genre by making innovations in the field of themes as well as techniques. It meets the challenges posed by both the Bhasa writers and postcolonial writers.

Indian English literature is rich in fiction, short story and poetry but poor in drama, autobiography, biography and non-fictional prose. Indian English Writers fulfil multi-cultural commitments. As they are familiar with literatures in English and foreign cultures through the writings of Anglo-American writers, they cease to be culturally insular. Edward Said makes a pertinent comment on this point when he says:

> No one today is purely one thing. Labels like Indian, or woman, or Muslim, of American are no more than starting points which, if followed into actual experience for only a moment, are quickly left behind. Imperialism consolidated the mixture of cultures and identities on a global scale. But its worst and most paradoxical gift was to allow people to belief that they were only, mainly exclusively white, or black, or Western, or Oriental.

> No one can deny the persisting continuities of long traditions, sustained habitations, natural languages, and cultural geographies, but there seems no reason except fear and prejudice, to keep insisting on their separation and distinctiveness as if that was all human life was about. Survival in fact is about connections between things; in Eliot's phrase, reality cannot be deprived of the "other echoes (that) inhabit the garden." It is more rewarding — and more difficult — to think correctly and sympathetically, contrapuntally, about others than only about "us." But this also means not trying to rule others, not trying to classify them or put them in hierarchies, above all not constantly reiterating "how our 'culture' or country is number one (or not number one, for that matter), for the intellectual there is quite enough of value to do without that" (1993:408).

Since Indian English writer combines in his writings the traits of the West as well as the East, he excels Bhasa writers at home and ranks among post-colonial writers abroad.

New generations of Indian English writers and the old writers who continue to write such as Mulk Raj Anand and Raja Rao, write in a new way, by experimenting with themes and idioms. Arundhati Roy's terms such as 'Biological father' (*i.e.*, the lover of one's mother, who is not legally married to her), 'disable age' (*i.e.*, the appropriate age of dying) are used freely in her novel. Indian English literature is a meeting point between the West and the East and therefore, it is a rich literature.

To conclude, I should say that Postmodern Indian English literature has a luxuriant growth. It has expanded both the themes and in techniques. Not only our writers are saying new things, but they are saying it in a new idiom that at once distinguishes them from post-colonial writers elsewhere. They have broadened the horizon of Indian English literature, and brought it closer to Third World Literature. Contemporary Indian English writers have contact with the 'live' language as most of them live half of the year abroad. Words obey their call, and they take all aspects of contemporary society 'as their province.' Indian English literature like any Bhasa literature is Indian in sensibility and expression. This reminds us of Raja Rao's prophecy that "we can't write like the English. We should not. We can't write only as Indians. We have grown to look at the large world as part of us. Our method of expression therefore has to be dialect which will someday prove to be as distinctive and colourful as the Irish or the American. Time alone will justify it." Time has already done so. Postmodern Indian English literature is at once a Pan Indian literature and part of post-colonial literature. Its future is immense.

Works Cited

Niven, Alstair. "Word for Word." *The Hindu Literary Review.* Sunday, 7 May 2000.

Rao, Raja. "Foreword." *Kanthapura.* Delhi: OUP, 1989.

Said, Edward. *Culture and Imperialism.* London: Chatto and Windus, 1993.

Select Bibliography

Albertazzi, Silvia. *Translating India: Travel and Cross-Cultural Transference in Post-Colonial Indian Friction in English*. Bologna: Editrice Bologna, 1993.

Amur, G.S. & S.K. Desai. Eds. *Colonial Consciousness in Commonwealth Literature: Essays Presented to Prof C.D. Narasimhaiah*. Bombay: Somaya Publications, 1984.

Amur, G.S. *et al.* Eds. Indian Readings in Commonwealth Literature. New Delhi: Sterling, 1985.

Ashcroft, Bill *et al.* Eds. *The Empire Writes Back: Theory and Practice in Post-Colonial Literatures*. London: Routledge, 1989.

Asnani, Shyam M. *Critical Responses to Indian English Fiction*. Delhi: Mittal Publications, 1986.

——. New Dimensions of Indian English Novel. Delhi: Doaba House, 1988.

Balaram Gupta, G.S. Ed. *Studies in Indian Fiction in English*. Gulbarga: JIWE Publications, 1987.

Bharucha, Nilufer E. & Vilas Sarang. Eds. *Indian English Fiction 1980-1990: An Assessment*. New Delhi: B.R. Publishing Corporation, 1994.

Bharucha, Nilufer & Vrinda Nabar. Eds. *Mapping Cultural Spaces: Post-Colonial Indian Literature in English*. New Delhi: Vision Books, 1998.

Bhatnagar, O.P. *Perspectives on Indian Poetry in English*. Amaravati: Bajaj Publications, 1986.

Bhatta, S. Krishna. *Indian English Drama: A Critical Study*. New Delhi: Sterling, 1987.

Bhattacharjee, Aditya & Lola Chatterjee. Ed. *The Fiction of St Stephen's*. New Delhi: Ravi Dayal, 2000.

Das, Bijay Kumar. *Critical Essays on Poetry:* Ludhiana: Kalyani Publishers, 1993.

——. Modern *Indo-English Poetry*. Bareilly: Prakash Book Depot, 1982.

——. *The Poetry of Jayanta Mahapatra*. New Delhi: Atlantic Publishers, 1995 (Enlarged Edition, 2001).

——. *The Horizon of Nissim Ezekiel's Poetry*. New Delhi: D.K. Publishers, 1995.

——. *Aspects of Commonwealth Literature*. New Delhi: Creative Books, 1995.
——. *Critical Essays on Post-colonial Literature*. New Delhi: Atlantic Publishers, 1999, 2001.
——. *Shiv K. Kumar as a Post-Colonial Poet*. New Delhi: Atlantic Publishers, 2001.
——. *A Reader's Guide to Ten Twentieth Century Indian Poets*. Barielly: Prakash Book Depot, 1999.
——. Ed. *Contemporary Indo-English Poetry*. Bareilly: PBD, 1986.
——. Ed. *Perspectives on the Poetry of R. Parthasarathy*. Bareilly: PBD, 1983, 1999.
Dasgupta, Swapan. Ed. *Nirad C. Choudhury: The First Hundred Years: A Celebration*. New Delhi: Harper Collins India, 1997. Dash, Sandhyarani. *Form and Vision in the Novels of Anita Desai*. New Delhi: Prestige, 1996.
Dass, Veena Noble & R.K. Dhawan. Ed. *Fiction of the Nineties*. New Delhi: Prestige, 1994.
Devy, G.N. *After Amnesia: Tradition and Change in Indian Literary Criticism*. Bombay: Orient Longman, 1992.
——. *"Of Many Heroes": An Indian Essay on Literary Historiography*.
Hyderabad: Orient Longman, 1998.
——. *Into Another Tongue: Essay on Indian English Literature*. Madras: MacMillan, 1995.
Dhanavel, P. *The Indian Imagination of Girish Karnad*. New Delhi: Prestige, 2000.
Dhawan, R.K. Ed. *Post-Colonial Discoursed Study in Contemporary Literature*. New Delhi: Prestige, 1997.
——. Ed. *The Novels of Mulk Raj Anand*. New Delhi: Prestige, 1992.
——. Ed. *Nirad C. Choudhury: The Scholar Extraordinary*. New Delhi: Prestige, 2000.
——. Ed. *The Fiction of Anita Desai*. Delhi: Bahri Publications, 1989.
——. Ed. *The Novels of Amitav Ghosh*. New Delhi: Prestige, 1999.
Dodiya, Jaydipsinh. *The Plays of Girish Karnad*. New Delhi: Prestige, 1999.
Dwivedi, A.N. Ed. *Contemporary Indo-English Verse: Male Poets*. Bareilly: Prakash Book Depot, 1984.
——. Ed. *Studies in Contemporary Indian Fiction in English*. Allahabad: Kitab Mahal, 1987.
——. Ed. *Studies in Contemporary Indian English Short Story*. New Delhi: B.R. Publishing Corporation, 1991.
——. *A Study of Sri Aurobindo's "Savitri" and Other Select Poems*. Bareilly: Prakash Book Depot, 1989.

——. *Toru Dutt: A Literary Profile.* New Delhi: B.R. Publishing Corporation, 1998.

Dwivedy, Suresh Chandra. Ed. *Perspectives on Nissim Ezekiel: Essays in Honour of Rosemary C. Wilkinson.* New Delhi: K.M. Agencies, 1989.

Hariprasanna, A. *The World of Malgudi: A Study of R.K. Narayan's Novels.* New Delhi: Prestige, 1994.

Harish, Ranjana. *Indian Women's Autobiographies.* New Delhi: Arnold Publishers, 1993.

Jain, Jasbir. *Nayantara Saghal.* Jaipur: Printwell, 1994.

——. *Problems of Post-Colonial Literatures and Other Essays.* Jaipur: Printwell, 1991.

——. Ed. *Women's Writting: Text and Context.* Jaipur: Rawat Publications, 1996.

Jena, Seema. *Voice and Vision of Anita Desai.* New Delhi: Ashish Publishing House, 1989.

Jha, Rekha. *The Novels of Kamala Markandaya and Ruthjhabvala: A Study in East-West Encounter.* New Delhi: Prestige, 1990.

Kanwar, Asha. *Virginia Woolf and Anita Desai: A Contemporary Study.* New Delhi: Prestige, 1989.

Karnani, Chetan. *Indian Writting in English.* New Delhi: Arnold Associates, 1995.

Khair, Tabish. *Babu Fictions: Alienation in Contemporary Indian English Novels.* New Delhi: OUP, 2000.

Khanna, Shashi. *Human Relationships in Anita Desai's Novels.* New Delhi: Samp & Sons, 1995.

King, Bruce. *Modern Indian Poetry in English.* New Delhi: OUP, 1987.

——. *Three Indian Poets: Nissim Ezekiel, A.K. Ramanujan, Dom Moraes.* New Delhi: OUP, 1991.

Kirpal, Viney. Ed. *The New Indian Novel in English: A Study of the 1980s.* New Delhi: Allied Publishers, 1990.

——. Ed. *The Postmodern Indian English Novel: Interrogating the 1980s and 1990s.* New Delhi: Allied Publishers, 1996.

Kulshreshtha, Chirantan. Ed. *Contemporary Indian English Verse: An Evaluation.* New Delhi: Arnold Heinemann, 1980.

Kumar, Shiv K. *Contemporary Indian Literature in English.* Shimla: Indian Institute of Advanced Study, 1992.

Lal, Malashri. *The Law of the Threshold: Women Writers in Indian English.* Shimla: Indian Institute of Advanced Study, 1995.

Lall, Emmanuel Narendra. *The Poetry of Encounter: Three Indo-Anglian Poets.* New Delhi: Sterling, 1983.

Manohar, D. Murali. Kamla Das: *Treatment of Love in Her Poetry.* Gulbarga: JIWE, 1999.

Mathur, O.P. *Modern Indian English Fiction.* Delhi: Abhinav Publications, 1993.

Mathur, O.P. *Indian Political Novel and Other Essays.* Allahabad: Kitab Mahal, 1995.

McLeod, A.L. *R.K. Narayan: Critical Perspectives.* New Delhi: Sterling, 1994.

Misra, D.S. *Contemporary English Poetry: A Revaluation.* Vallabh Vidyanagar: Sardar Patel Univ., 1991.

Mohan, Devinder. *Jayanta Mahapatra.* New Delhi: Arnold Heinemann, 1987.

Mohanty, Seemita. *Dimensions of Suitability: A Study of Vikram Seth's "A Suitable Boy."* Cuttack: Arya Prakashan, 1997.

Mukherjee, Meenakshi. *Realism and Reality: The Novel and Society in India.* New Delhi: OUP, 1985.

——. *The Perishable Empire: Essays on Indian Writting in English.*
New Delhi: OUP, 2000.

——. Ed. *Rushdie's 'Midnight's Children': A Book of Readings.* New Delhi: Pencraft, 1999.

Nabar, Vrinda. Endless Female Hungers: A Study of Kamala Das. New Delhi: Sterling, 1993.

Nagarajan, M.S. *et al.* Eds. *Essays in Criticism on Indian Literature in English.* Delhi: S. Chand, 1991.

Nahal, Chaman. *The New Literatures in English.* New Delhi: Allied, 1995.

Nandakumar, Prema. *Aurobindo: A Critical Introduction.* New Delhi: Sterling, 1998.

Naik, M.K. *A History of Indian English Literature.* New Delhi: Sahitya Akademi, 1982.

——. *Dimensions of Indian English Literature.* New Delhi: Sterling, 1984.

——. Ed. *Perspectives on Indian Fiction in English.* New Delhi: Abhinav Publications, 1985.

——. Ed. *Perspective on Indian Poetry in English.* Abhinav Publications, 1998.

Naik, M.K. and Shyamala A. Narayan. *Indian English Literature, 1980-2000: A Critical Study.* New Delhi: Pencraft, 2001.

Nair, K.R. Ramachandran. *Three Indo-Anglian Poets.* New Delhi: Sterling, 1987.

Nanavati, U.M. and P.C. Kar. *Rethinking Indian English Literature.* New Delhi: Pencraft, 2000.

Narasimhaiah, C.D. Commonwealth Literature: Heirloom of Multiple Heritage. New Delhi: Pencraft, 1995.

——. *The Swan and the Eagle: Essays on Indian English Literature.* Shimla: Indian Institute of Advanced Study & Delhi: Motilal Banarasi Das, 1987.
——. Ed. *Makers of Indian English Literature.* New Delhi: Pencraft, 2000.
Pandey, Mukteswar. *Arun Joshi: The Existential Elements in His Novels.* New Delhi: B.R. Publishing Co., 1998.
Pandey, Sudhakar. Ed. *New Directions in Indian Drama.* New Delhi: Prestige, 1994.
——. Eds. *Studies in Contemporary Indian Drama. New Delhi:* Prestige, 1990.
Pande, Sudhakar & R.Raj Rao. Eds. *The Image of Indian in the Indian Novel in English 1969-1985.* Hyderabad: Orient Longman, 1993.
Pandey, Surya Nath. Ed. *Nissim Ezekiel: Dimensions of a Poetic Genius.* New Delhi: Doaba House, 1999.
Panikar, K. Ayappa. Ed. *Contemporary Indian Fiction in English.* Trivandrum: University of Kerala, 1987.
Parameswaran, Uma, *Kamala Markandaya.* Jaipur: Rawat Publications, 2000.
Paranjape, Markanda. *Nativism: Essays in Criticism.* New Delhi: Sahitya Akademi, 1997.
——. *Mysticism in Indian English Poetry.* Delhi: B.R. Publishing, 1988.
——. *Towards a Poetics of the Indian English Novel.* Shimla: Indian Institute of Advanced Study, 2000.
Pathak, R.S. Ed. *Indian Fiction in English: Problems and Promises.* New Delhi: Northern Block Centre, 1990.
——. *Ed. Quest For Identity in Indian English Writing.* New Delhi: Bahri Publications, 1992.
——. Ed. *Recent Indian Fiction.* New Delhi: Prestige, 1994.
Perry, John Oliver. Absent Authority: Issues in Contemporary Indian English Criticism. New Delhi: Sterling, 1992.
Punekar, Shankar Mokashi. *Post-Independence Indo-English Poetry.* Calcutta: Writers Workshop, 1998.
Prasad, H.M. Ed. *Indian Poetry in English.* Aurangabad: Parimal Prakashan, 1983.
——. Ed. *Response: Recent Revaluation of Indian Fiction in English.* Bareilly: Prakash Book Depot, 1984.
——. Arun Joshi. New Delhi: Arnold Heinemann, 1986.
Prasad, M.S. Ed. *Indian English Novelists: An Anthology of Critical Essays.* New Delhi: Sterling, 1982.
Radha, K. Kamala Das. Mardas: MacMillan India, 1987.
Rahaman, Anisur. *Expressive Form in the Poetry of Kamala Das.* New Delhi: Abhinav Publications, 1981.

——. *Form and Value in the Poetry of Nissim Ezekiel. New* Delhi: Abhinav Publications, 1981.

Raja, P. *The Many Worlds of Manoj Das* New Delhi: D.K. Publishing Co., 1993.

Rajan, P.K. Ed. *Changing Tradition in Indian English Literature.* New Delhi: Creative Books, 1995.

Ram, Atma. *Contemporary Indian English Poetry.* Calcutta: Writers' Workshop, 1989.

——. *Essays on Indian English Literature.* Aurangabad: Parimal, 1984.

——. *Indian Poetry and Fiction in English.* New Delhi: Bahri Publications, 1991.

Ramaswamy, S. *Commentaries on Commonwealth Poetry and Drama.* New Delhi: Prestige, 1994.

——. *Commentaries on Commonwealth Fiction.* New Delhi: Prestige, 1994.

——. *Explorations: Essays on Commonwealth Literature.* Bangalore: M.C.C. Publications, 1988.

Rao, C.M. Mohan. *Manohar Malgonkar and Portrait of the Hero in his Novels.* New Delhi: Reliance, 1993.

Rao, R. Raj. *Nissim Ezekiel: The Authorised Biography.* New Delhi: Viking-Penguin India, 2000.

Reddy, P. Bayappa. *Studies in Indian Writing in English with a Focuss on Indian English Drama.* New Delhi: Prestige, 1990.

——. *The Plays of Arif Currimbhoy.* Calcutta: Writers' Workshop, 1986.

Saha, S.C. *Indian Renaissance and Indian English Poetry.* New Delhi: Prestige, 1998.

Satchidanandan, K. *Indian Literature: Positions and Propositions.* New Delhi: Pencraft, 1999.

Sandhu, Sarbajit. *The Image of Woman in the Novels of Shashi Deshpande.* New Delhi: Prestige, 1991.

Shahane, V.A. & M. Shivaramakrishna. Ed. *Indian Poetry in English: A Critical Assessment.* Madras: Macmillan, 1980.

Sharma, R.S. & Shashi Bala Talwar. Ed. *Arundhati Roy's God of Small Things:* Critique and Commentary. New Delhi: Creative Books, 1998.

Sharma, T.R. Ed. *Essays on Nissim Ezekiel.* Meerut: Salabh Prakashan, 1994.

Singh, Amar K. *Enlightening Studies in Indian English Poetry.* New Delhi: Manak Publications, 1994.

Singh, Avadesh K. Ed. *Contemporary Fiction in English.* New Delhi: Creative Books, 1994.

Singh, R.A. *Keki N. Daruwalla: Assessment as a Poet.* Bareilly: Prakash Book Depot, 1992.

Singh, Sunaina. *The Novels of Margaret Atwood and Anita Desai: A Comparative Study in Feminist Perspective.* New Delhi: Creative Books, 1994.

Sinha, Ravi Nandan & R.K. Sinha. Ed. *The Indian Novel in English: Essays in Criticism.* Ranchi: Ankit Publishers, 1987.

Solanki, Mrinalini. *Anita Desai's Fiction: Patterns of Survival Strategies.* New Delhi: Kanishka Publishing, 1992.

Srinath, C.N. *The Commonwealth Novel: A Study of the Comic Mode and the Theme of Success.* Bangalore: Prasaranga Bangalore Univ., 1997.

Srivastava, A.K. Ed. *Alien Voice: Perspectives on Commonwealth Literatures.* Lucknow: Pring House, 1981.

Srivastava, R.K. *Perspectives on Anita Desai.* Ghaziabad: Vimal Prakashan, 1985.

Trivedi, Harish & M. Mukherjee. Ed. *Interrogating Post- Colonialism: Theory, Text and Context.* Shimla: Indian Institute of Advanced Study, 1996.

Varma, R.M. *Some Aspects of Indo-English Fiction.* New Delhi: Jaisons Publications, 1985.

Viswanathan, Gauri. *Masks of Conquest: Literary Study and English Rule in India.* London: Faber, 1990.

Walsh, William. *Indian Literature in English.* London: Longman, 1990.

Index